Self-portrait Wearing a Fur-trimmed Coat. 1500. Oil on wood.

Dürer's Record of Journeys to Venice and the Low Countries

ALBRECHT DÜRER

Edited by Roger Fry

DOVER PUBLICATIONS, INC.
New York

Bibliographical Note

This Dover edition, first published in 1995, is an unabridged republication of the work originally published by The Merrymount Press, Boston, in 1913 under the title *Records of Journeys to Venice and the Low Countries* (Vol. VI of The Humanist's Library, edited by Lewis Einstein). A selection of illustrations of works by Albrecht Dürer have been added to the Dover edition.

Library of Congress Cataloging-in-Publication Data

Dürer, Albrecht, 1471–1528.
    [Correspondence. English. Selections]
    Dürer's Record of journeys to Venice and the Low Countries / Albrecht Dürer ; edited by Roger Fry.
    p.   cm.
    Originally published: Records of journeys to Venice and the Low Countries. Boston : Merrymount Press, 1913. With new ill.
    Contents: Letters from Venice to Wilibald Pirkheimer — Diary of a journey in the Netherlands — Notes
    ISBN 0-486-28348-8 (pbk.)
    1. Dürer, Albrecht, 1471–1528—Correspondence. 2. Artists—Germany—Correspondence. 3. Pirckheimer, Willibald, 1470–1530—Correspondence. 4. Dürer, Albrecht, 1471–1528—Diaries. 5. Artists—Germany—Diaries. 6. Dürer, Albrecht, 1471–1528—Journeys. 7. Venice (Italy)—Description and travel. 8. Netherlands—Description and travel. I. Fry, Roger Eliot, 1866–1934. II. Dürer, Albrecht, 1471–1528. Tagebuch der Reise in die Niederlande. English. 1995. III. Title. IV. Title: Record of journeys to Venice and the Low Countries.
N6888.D8A3   1995
760'.092—dc20
[B]
                    94-44870
                    CIP

Manufactured in the United States of America
Dover Publications, Inc., 31 East 2nd Street, Mineola, N.Y. 11501

A TABLE OF CONTENTS

LIST OF ILLUSTRATIONS

INTRODUCTION

*** *
*

I T is a habit of the human mind to make to itself symbols in order to abbreviate its admiration for a class. So Dürer has come to stand
for German art somewhat as Raphael once stood
for that of Italy. Such symbols attract to themselves much of the adoration which more careful worshippers would distribute over the Pan-
theon, and it becomes difficult to appreciate
them justly without incurring the charge of icon-
oclasm. It is the more difficult in Dürer's case because, whatever one's final estimate of his art,
his personality is at once so imposing and so
attractive, and has been so endeared to us by
familiarity, that something of this personal at-
tachment has been transferred to our aesthetic
judgement.

The letters from Venice and the Diary of his
journey in the Netherlands, which form the contents of this volume, are indeed the singularly
fortunate means for this pleasant intercourse with
the man himself. They reveal Dürer as one of
the distinctively modern men of the Renaissance:
intensely, but not arrogantly, conscious of his own
personality; accepting with a pleasant ease the
universal admiration of his genius,—a personal

admiration, too, of an altogether modern kind; careful of his fame as one who foresaw its immortality. They show him as having, though in a far less degree, something of Leonardo da Vinci's scientific interest, certainly as possessing a quick, though naïve curiosity about the world and a quite modern freedom from superstition. It is clear that his dominating and yet kindly personality, no less than his physical beauty and distinction, made him the centre of interest wherever he went. His easy and humorous good-fellowship, of which the letters to Pirkheimer are eloquent, won for him the admiring friendship of the best men of his time. To all these characteristics we must add a deep and sincere religious feeling, which led him to side with the leaders of the Reformation, a feeling which comes out in his passionate sense of loss when he thinks that Luther is about to be put to death, and causes him to write a stirring letter to Erasmus, urging him to continue the work of reform. For all that, there is no trace in him of either Protestantism or Puritanism. He was perhaps fortunate—certainly as an artist he was fortunate—to live at a time when the line of cleavage between the reformers and the Church was not yet so marked as to compel a decisive action. The symbolism of the Church still had for him its old significance, as yet quickened and not discredited by the reformer's energy. But intense as Dürer's devotion was, this religious feeling

viii

scarcely found its way to effective artistic expression upon one side, namely, the brooding sense which accompanied it of the imminence and terror of death. How much more definite is the inspiration in the drawing of Death on a horse (in the British Museum), in the Knight Death and the Devil, and in the allied Melancholia, than it is in his renderings of the Virgin or indeed of any of the scenes of Christian legend! It is this feeling, too, which gives to his description of his mother's death its almost terrible literary beauty and power.

Nor in the estimate of Dürer's character must one leave out the touching affection and piety which the family history written by him in 1524 reveals. So much that is attractive and endearing in the man cannot but react upon our attitude to his work—has done so, perhaps, ever since his own day; and it is difficult to get far enough away from Dürer the man to be perfectly just to Dürer the artist. But if we make the attempt, it becomes clear, I think, that Dürer cannot take rank in the highest class of creative geniuses. His position is none the less of great importance and interest for his relation on the one hand to the Gothic tradition of his country, and on the other to the newly perceived splendour of the Italian Renaissance. Much must depend on our estimate of his last work, the "Four Apostles," at Munich. In that he summed up all that the patient and enthusiastic labour of a lifetime had taught him. If we regard

that as a work of the highest beauty, if we can
conscientiously put it beside the figures of the
Sistine Chapel, beside the Saints of Mantegna, or
Signorelli, or Piero della Francesca, then indeed
Dürer's labour was crowned with success; but if
we find in it rather a careful exposition of certain
theoretical principles, if we find that the matter
is not entirely transfused with the style, if we find
a conflict between a certain naïve crudity of vision and a straining after the grand manner, then
we have to say that Dürer's art was the outcome
of a magnificent and heroic but miscalculated
endeavour.

It is among the ironies of history that the Ro-
mans, the one Philistine people among the Me-
diterranean races, should have been the great
means of transmitting to the modern world that
culture which they themselves deposed, and that
the Germans should have laboured so long and
hard to atone for the heroism of their ancestors
in resisting that beneficent loss of liberty. Nuremberg of the fifteenth century was certainly given
over to the practice of fine art with a pathetic en-
thusiasm, and it remains as a sad but instructive
proof of how little good-will and industry avail by
themselves in such matters. The worship of mere
professional skill and undirected craftsmanship is
there seen pushed to its last conclusions, and the
tourist's wonder is excited by the sight of stone
carved into the shapes of twisted metal, and wood

simulating the intricacies of confectionery, his admiration is canvassed by every possible perver-
sion of technical dexterity. Not, "What a thing is
done!" but, "How difficult it must have been to
do it!" is the exclamation demanded.

Of all that perverted technical ingenuity which
flaunts itself in the wavering stonework of a Kraft
or the crackling woodwork of a Storr, Dürer was
inevitably the heir. He grew up in an atmosphere
where the acrobatic feats of technique were
looked on with admiration rather than contempt.
Something of this clung to him through life, and
he is always recognized as the prince of craftsmen, the consummate technician. In all this side
of Dürer's art we recognize the last over-blown
efflorescence of the mediaeval craftsmanship of
Germany, of the apprentice system and the
"marker" piece; but that Gothic tradition had still
left in it much that was sound and sincere. Drawing still retained something of the blunt, almost
brutal frankness of statement, together with the
sense of the characteristic which marked its earlier
period. And it is perhaps this inheritance of Gothic
directness of statement, this Gothic realism, that
accounts for what is ultimately of most value
in Dürer's work. There exists in the Kunsthisto-
risches Akademie at Vienna a portrait of a man,
dated 1394, which shows how much of Dürer's
portraiture was already endemic in the Nuremberg school. Indeed, in this remarkable work, exe-

cuted, if we may trust the date, nearly a century
before Dürer, there is almost everything that interests us in Dürer's portraits. It has to an even
greater extent that half-humorous statement of
the characteristic, that outrageous realism that
makes the vivid appeal of the "Oswold Kroll,"
and the absence of which in Dürer's last years
makes the "Holzschuher" such a tiresome piece
of brilliant delineation.

Dürer was perhaps the greatest infant prod-
igy among painters, and the drawing of himself at the age of twelve shows how early he
had marked that simple and abrupt sincerity of
Gothic draughtsmanship. One is inclined to say
that in all his subsequent work he never surpassed
this in all that really matters, in all that concerns
the essential vision and its adequate presentment.
He increased his skill until it became the wonder
of the world and entangled him in its seductions;
his intellectual apprehension was indefinitely
heightened, and his knowledge of natural appear-
ances became encyclopaedic.

What, then, lies at the root of Dürer's art is this
Gothic sense of the characteristic, already men-
aced by the professional bravura of the late
Gothic craftsman. The superstructure is what
Dürer's industry and intellectual acquisitiveness,
acting in the peculiar conditions of his day,
brought forth. It is in short what distinguishes
him as the pioneer of the Renaissance in Ger-

many. This new endeavour was in two directions,
one due mainly to the trend of native ideas,
the other to Italian influence. The former was
concerned mainly with a new kind of realism. In
place of the older Gothic realism with its naïve
and self-confident statement of the salient characteristic of things seen, this new realism strove at
complete representation of appearance by means
of perspective, at a more searching and complete
investigation of form, and a fuller relief in light
and shade.

These aims were also followed to some extent
by the Italians, and with even greater scientific
ardour: all the artists of Europe were indeed striv-
ing to master the complete power of representation. But in Italy this aim was never followed
exclusively; it was constantly modified and con-
trolled by the idea of design, that is to say, of expression by means of the pure disposition of con-
tours and masses, and by the perfection and or-
dering of linear rhythm. This notion of design as
something other than representation was indeed
the common inheritance of European art from
the mediaeval world, but in Italy the principles
of design were more profoundly embedded in
tradition, its demands were more clearly felt, and
each succeeding generation was quite as deeply
concerned with the perfection of design as with
the mastery of representation. In the full Renaissance, indeed, this idea of design became the ob-

ject of extremely conscious and deliberate study, and the decadence of Italian art came about, not through indifference to the claims of artistic expression, but through a too purely intellectual and conscious study of them. The northern and especially the Teutonic artists, who had not inherited so strongly this architectonic sense, made indeed heroic efforts to acquire it, sometimes by the futile method of direct imitation of a particular style, sometimes – and this is the case with Dürer – by a serious effort of aesthetic intelligence. But on the whole the attempt must be judged to have failed, and northern art has drifted gradually towards the merely photographic vision.

Dürer strove strenuously in both these directions. He unquestionably added immensely to the knowledge of actual form and to the power of representation, but his eagerness led him to regard the quantity of form rather than its quality. With him drawing became a means of making manifest the greatest possible amount of form, the utmost roundness of relief, and his studies in pure design failed to keep pace with this. In the end he could not use to significant purpose the increased material at his disposal, and from the point of view of pure design his work actually falls short of his predecessor, Martin Schongauer's, who indeed was benefited by lacking Dürer's power of representation.

From this point of view it may be worth while

to examine in some detail Dürer's relations to Italian art. The earliest definite example of his study
of Italian art is in 1494, when he was probably in
Venice for the first time. It is a copy in pen and
ink of an engraving of the "Death of Orpheus" by
some follower of Mantegna. The engraving is not
the work of a great artist, and Dürer's copy shows
his superior skill in the rendering of form; but
even here he has failed to realize the beauty of
spatial arrangement in the original, and his desire
to enrich the design with many skilfully drawn
and convincing details results in a distinct weak-
ening of the dramatic effect. Again, in the same
year we have two drawings from engravings,
this time by Mantegna himself. It is easy to understand that of all Italians, Mantegna should
have been the most sympathetic to Dürer, and
that he regretted more than any other ill-fortune
of his life, – more even than the similar fate that
prevented his meeting Schongauer, – Mantegna's
death just when he was setting out to Mantua to
learn from the great master. What Dürer saw in
Mantegna was his clear decision of line and his
richly patterned effect. In his pen and ink copies
he tries to surpass the original in both these ways,
and indeed the effect is of greater complexity,
more fullness and roundness of form. Where
Mantegna is content with a firm statement of
the generalized contour of a limb, Dürer will give
a curve for each muscle. There is in Dürer's copies

a mass of brilliant detail, each part is in a sense
more convincingly real; but in doing this something of the unity of rhythm and the easy relations of planes has been lost, and on the whole
the balance is against the copyist. It is curious
that when in time Rembrandt came to copy
Mantegna he took the other way, and actually
heightened the dramatic effect by minute read-
justments of design, and by a wilful simplifica-
tion of the line.

Dürer evidently felt a profound reverence for
Mantegna's designs, for he has altered them but
little, and one might well imagine that even Dürer
could scarcely improve upon such originals. But
it is even more instructive to study his modifica-
tions of the so-called Tarrochi engravings. Here
the originals probably were not executed by an
artist of first-rate ability, though the designs have
much of Cossa's splendid style. Dürer seems
therefore to have felt no particular constraint
about altering them. His changes show us clearly
what it was that he saw in the originals and
what he missed. In all these figures Dürer gives
increased verisimilitude: his feet are like actual
feet, not the schematic abstract of a foot that
contents the Italian engraver; his poses are more
casual, less formal and symmetrical; and his dra-
peries are more ingeniously disposed; but none
the less, from the point of view of the expression
of imaginative truth, there is not one of Dürer's

figures which equals the original, not one in which some essential part of the idea is not missed or at least less clearly stated. In general the continuity of the contour is lost sight of and the rhythm frittered away. In the Pope, for instance, Dürer loses all the grave sedateness of the original by breaking the symmetry of the pose, its squareness and immovable aplomb. And with this goes, in spite of the increased verisimilitude, the sense of reality. In the knight and page not only is the movement of the knight missed by correcting a distortion in the original, but the balance of the composition is lost by displacing the page. In the Primum Mobile the ecstatic rush of the figure is lost by slight corrections of the pose and by giving to the floating drapery too complicated a design. It would be tedious to go through these copies in detail, but enough has been said to show how hard it was for Dürer, absorbed by the new curiosity in representation, to grasp those primary and elemental principles of design which seem inherent in the Italian tradition.

About the same time we find Dürer studying both Pollajuolo and Lorenzo di Credi. The copy of Pollajuolo is not a good example of Dürer's art, it certainly misses the tension and inner life of Pollajuolo's nudes. The Lorenzo di Credi, as might be expected, is in many ways more than adequate to the original, though as compared even with Credi, Dürer has not a clear sense of

the correlation of linear elements in the design.
The next stage in Dürer's connection with Italian art is his intimacy with Jacopo de' Barbari,
who was settled in Nuremberg. From 1500 to 1505
this influence manifests itself clearly in Dürer's
work. Unfortunately Barbari was too second-rate
an artist to help Dürer much in the principles
of design, though he doubtless stimulated him
to pursue those scientific investigations into the
theory of human proportions which held out the
delusive hope of reducing art to a branch of
mathematics.

The next incident in the story is the second
visit to Venice, when Dürer realized at all events
the inferiority of Barbari, and through his ami-
able relations with Giovanni Bellini came nearer
than at any other moment of his life to penetrating the mysteries of Italian design. The letters
from Venice themselves throw so interesting a
light on his connection with the Venetian artists
of his day that it will be best to turn at once to
them to see what light they throw on Dürer's
artistic consciousness, how he regarded his own
work when seen in comparison with that of the
Venetians, and in what light the Venetians regarded this wonder worker from the north.

To those who have derived their ideas of travel
in the later Middle Ages from Charles Reade's
"Cloister and the Hearth," with its atmosphere
of romance and mystery, its exciting adventures

and hairbreadth escapes, Dürer's journal of the
visit to the Netherlands must seem but a very
tame every-day record. The diary indeed betrays
little more anxiety as to safety or even con-
venience than one of our own time might. The
undertaking scarcely seems as serious as a coach
journey in eighteenth century England when
travellers still congratulated themselves on passing Hounslow Heath in safety. The fact is that
travelling in the sixteenth century was by no
means the difficult and exceptional undertaking
which we are accustomed to picture it to ourselves; certainly the main routes of travel presented no great difficulties; it was only in Spain that
the diaries of that age reveal actual danger and
acute discomfort. No doubt, however, a change
had come with the beginning of the Renaissance,
but even this was rather a change in the attitude
of the traveller than in the conveniences of travel
itself. The change which we notice in comparing
Dürer's diary with earlier ones consists in this,
that his attitude as a traveller is essentially modern, that what he looks at in foreign countries is
the same as that to which Baedeker now guides
us, whereas throughout the Middle Ages and until
just before Dürer's time the traveller's journey
was punctuated only by his visits to places of
pilgrimage. Only half a century earlier the much
travelled Leo von Rozmithal saw things which
would strike a false note in Dürer's journal. At

Beaugency on the Loire he and his companions
saw a woman and her child fall into the Loire and
reappear two miles lower down, having traversed
the distance entirely under water by miraculous
aid and without any harm. On the confines of
Spain and Portugal he passed through a valley
which was filled with large winged dragons. With
him, too, the chief interest of travel consisted in
the visit to places of pilgrimage. The stars of a fifteenth century Baedeker would certainly have
been judiciously distributed among those relics
whose authenticity could be absolutely guaran-
teed. In contrasting the two thus, Dürer is as modern as his contemporary Erasmus, and in the very
modernity and commonplaceness of his journal
lies its interest as a document of the life of the
Renaissance. Erasmus, it is true, gives a picture
of the German inns of the day which is by no
means pleasing, and which, if it is not partly a
result of extreme sensibility and a vivid literary
style, would suggest that Dürer, Frau Agnes, and
the maid Susanna may have suffered extremi-
ties of discomfort over which the diary passes in
silence; but the whole tone of the journal, with
its careful record of the minutest expenses, suggests as assurance an absence of all difficulty and
anxiety which is consoling. Dürer's painful an-
ticipations seem indeed to have been confined
entirely to the question of how to pass cheaply
through the innumerable customs with which the

Rhine banks were studded, and even here offi-
cialism seems to have been thoroughly well or-
ganized. The letter from the Bishop of Bamberg
which he carried, relieved him instantly of all
trouble and expense, and the record of his un-
failing exemption from dues becomes almost
monotonous.

As compared with the letters from Venice, the
journal indicates, perhaps, some change in Dürer's
character. Certainly years have told upon him;
the seclusion in Nuremberg, and perhaps his
daily intercourse with a woman whom we have
good reason to believe was narrow in her sym-
pathies, vulgar in her ambitions, and inclined to
avarice, have broken the gaiety and elasticity of
his nature, have made him somewhat tiresome
in his care for detail, especially where money is
concerned, until we have the impression of his
being almost fussy. One wishes that Dürer were
not quite so good a bourgeois; that instead of
keeping his accounts quite so accurately, he had
given to posterity a little more of his speculative
interest and curiosity in the problems of art and
life. Had advancing age, one wonders, really
crushed these out? It is impossible to imagine Leonardo da Vinci, whom in some ways Dürer re-
sembles, passing through so many strange lands
without noting a hundred odd or curious phe-
nomena which might stimulate his speculative
activity. Dürer shows himself here, as always, a

man of attractive character and dominating personality; for all his carefulness in money matters,
he is magnanimous and even generous. He rises
to every occasion with an easy grace of manner,
an innate tact and readiness. Through these mea-
gre details we obtain a picture of his imposing
personality, of the way he dominated his company. We feel that of all the great men that the
burghers of Antwerp had entertained, none had
accepted their sumptuous hospitality with better grace and more genial manners. Dürer retains
indeed much of his curiosity, but it seems often
a little misplaced, a little too naïve, and we can
hardly restrain a feeling of disappointment at the
relative values he attaches to things. What was
a man like Dürer doing with so many childish
curiosities in his trunks, the sugar canes, and the
many buffalo horns, and how comes it, with such
a bent for collection, we hear so little of Flemish works of art? But what interests us perhaps
most in the diary is his relations to the painters
of Flanders. He is evidently more at home with
them than he was with the Venetians. There is no
suggestion here of rivalry or antagonism; there
are no hints of the possibility of assassination.
This was perhaps natural,—apart from the fact
that Dürer came to Flanders with a world-wide
and established reputation,—for Flemish and German artists had so much in common in their
tradition, that there would be no bar to their

mutual admiration. Even at this advanced stage of his career Dürer seems to have remained open to impressions, still able to learn something from other artists, and once more, as in Venice, we can trace in the work of the period the quickening influence of a centre of artistic culture more vital than his own country could afford.

Many of the portrait drawings which he records in the journal have come down to us, and they all betray something of the influence upon him of Flemish art; even more, however, is this traceable in the painted portraits of the time, in the "Bernhard van Orley" at Dresden, and in the "Hans Imhof" of the Prado. The spacing of these pictures, the planning of the pattern of head and hat within the picture-space, show a breadth and a sense of volume which are not to be found in the compositions done at Nuremberg. Even in the handling of these two portraits we see that Dürer gained appreciably from being thrown once more with real masters of the painters' craft. Once again he becomes appreciably more of a painter, amplifies the planes, and suppresses something of unnecessary detail, and though he never returns to the splendid envelopment and richness of colour of "The Venetian Lady," he manages just at this period to mitigate his habitual tendency to tightness and thinness of design. There is nothing in either of these of the overemphatic realization of form, such as we find later

on in the "Jakob Muffel" or the "Holzschuher."
The influence was, moreover, reciprocal. Dürer's
influence by means of his engravings had of
course long penetrated to the Netherlands, but I
think it is not impossible in one or two instances to
trace evidence of the more intimate effect which
the visit of so striking a personality was likely to
make. In particular the "Portrait of Carondelet,"
by Mabuse, in the Louvre shows an approach
to Dürer's method both of design and modelling
which is not to be found either in earlier or later
works by that master. Even the technique with
its repetition of hatched lines suggests an exper-
iment in Dürer's more linear method, a renun-
ciation for the moment by Mabuse of the true
Netherlandish style of handling paint.

Besides the pictures and the many portrait
drawings of this period, the journal is illustrated
throughout by Dürer's sketch-book, scattered
leaves of which have so fortunately come down
to us.

Roger Fry

LETTERS FROM VENICE TO
WILIBALD PIRKHEIMER

Wil[l]ibald Pirkheimer. 1503. Charcoal.

LETTERS FROM VENICE TO WILIBALD PIRKHEIMER

* *
*

Venice, 6th January, 1506

To the Honourable and wise Wilibald Pirkheimer, in Nuremberg.

MY dear Master, To you and all yours, many happy good New Years. My willing service to you, dear Herr Pirkheimer. Know that I am in good health; may God send you better even than that. Now as to what you commissioned me, namely, to buy a few pearls and precious stones—you must know that I can find nothing good enough or worth the money; everything is snapped up by the Germans. Those who go about on the Riva always expect four times the value for anything, for they are the falsest knaves that live there. No one expects to get an honest service of them. For that reason some good people warned me to be on my guard against them. They told me that they cheat both man and beast, and that you could buy better things for less money at Frankfort than at Venice. As for the books which I was to order for you, Imhof has already seen to it, but if you are in need of anything else, let me know, and I shall do it for you with all zeal. And would to God that I could do you some real good service. I should gladly accomplish it, since I know how much you do for me. And I beg of you be patient with my debt, for I think oftener of it than you do. As soon as God helps me to get home I will pay you honourably, with many thanks; for I have to paint a picture for the Germans, for which they are giving me 110 Rhenish gulden, which will not cost me as much as five. I shall have finished laying and scraping the ground-work in eight days, then I shall at once begin to paint, and if God will, it shall be in its place for the altar a month after Easter.

The money I hope, if God will, to put by; and from that I will pay you: for I think that I need not send my mother and wife any money at present; I left 10 florins with my mother when I came away; she has since got 9 or 10 florins by selling works of art. Dratzieher has paid her 12 florins, and I have sent her 9 florins by Sebastian Imhof, of which she has to pay Pfinzing and Gartner 7 florins for rent. I gave my wife 12 florins and she got 13 more at Frankfort, making all together 25 florins, so I don't think she will be in any need, and if she does want anything, her brother will have to help her, until I come home, when I will repay him honourably. Herewith let me commend myself to you.

Given at Venice on the day of the Holy Three
Kings (Epiphany), the year 1506.
Greet for me Stephen Paumgartner and my
other good friends who ask after me.

Albrecht Dürer.

II

7th February, 1506

FIRST my willing service to you, dear Master. If it is well with you, I am as wholeheartedly glad as I should be for myself. I wrote to you recently. I hope the letter reached you. In the meantime my mother has written to me, chiding me for not writing to you, and has given me to understand that you are displeased with me because I do not write to you; and that I must excuse myself to you fully. And she is much worried about it, as is her wont. Now I do not know what excuse to make, except that I am lazy about writing and that you have not been at home. But as soon as I knew that you were at home or were coming home, I wrote to you at once; I also specially charged Castel (Fugger) to convey my service to you. Therefore I most humbly beg you to forgive me, for I have no other friend on earth but you; but I do not believe you are angry with me, for I hold you as no other than a father.

How I wish you were here at Venice, there are so many good fellows among the Italians who seek my company more and more every day — which is very gratifying to me — men of sense, and scholarly, good lute-players, and pipers, connoisseurs in painting, men of much noble sentiment and honest virtue, and they show me much honour and friendship. On the other hand, there are also amongst them the most faithless, lying, thievish rascals; such as I scarcely believed could exist on earth; and yet if one did not know them, one would think that they were the nicest men on earth. I cannot help laughing to myself when they talk to me: they know that their villainy is well known, but that does not bother them. I have many good friends among the Italians who warn me not to eat and drink with their painters, for many of them are my enemies and copy my work in the churches and wherever they can find it; afterwards they criticise it and claim that it is not done in the antique style and say it is no good, but Giambellin (Giovanni Bellini) has praised me highly to many gentlemen. He would willingly have something of mine, and came himself to me and asked me to do something for him, and said that he would pay well for it, and everyone tells me what an upright man he is, so that I am really friendly with him. He is very old and yet he is the best painter of all.

And the thing which pleased me so well eleven

years ago pleases me no longer, and if I had not seen it myself, I would not have believed anyone who told me. And you must know too that there are many better painters here than Master Jacob (Jacopo de' Barbari), though Antonio Kolb would take an oath that there was no better painter on earth than Jacob. Others sneer at him and say if he were any good, he would stay here. I have only to-day begun the sketch of my picture, for my hands are so scabby that I could not work, but I have cured them. And now be lenient with me and do not get angry so quickly, but be gentle like me. You will not learn from me, I do not know why. My dear, I should like to know whether any of your loves is dead—that one close by the water, for instance, or the one like [flower] or [tassel] or [dog] 's girl so that you might get another in her stead.

Given at Venice at the ninth hour of the night on Saturday after Candlemas in the year 1506.

Give my service to Stephen Paumgartner and to Masters Hans Harsdorfer and Volkamer.

Albrecht Dürer.

28th February, 1506

FIRST my willing service to you, dear Herr Pirkheimer. If things go well with you, then I am indeed glad. Know, too, that by the grace of God I am doing well and working fast. Still I do not expect to have finished before Whitsuntide. I have sold all my pictures except one. For two I got 24 ducats, and the other three I gave for these three rings, which were valued in the exchange as worth 24 ducats, but I have shown them to some good friends and they say they are only worth 22, and as you wrote to me to buy you some jewels, I thought that I would send you the rings by Franz Imhof. Show them to people who understand them, and if you like them, keep them for what they are worth. In case you do not want them, send them back by the next messenger, for here at Venice a man who helped to make the exchange will give me 12 ducats for the emerald and 10 ducats for the ruby and diamond, so that I need not lose more than 2 ducats.

I wish you had occasion to come here, I know the time would pass quickly, for there are so many nice men here, real artists. And I have such a crowd of foreigners (Italians) about me that I am forced sometimes to shut myself up, and the gentlemen all wish me well, but few of the painters.

Smiling Peasant Woman. 1505. Pen.
(A Slovenian woman drawn by Dürer on his way to Venice.)

Portrait of a Young Venetian Girl. 1505. Oil on wood.

Dear Master, Andreas Künhofer sends you his
service and means to write to you by the next
courier. Herewith let me be commended to you,
and I also commend my mother to you. I am won-
dering greatly why she has not written to me
for so long, and as for my wife, I begin to think
that I have lost her, and I am surprised too that
you do not write to me, but I have read the letter which you wrote to Sebastian Imhof about
me. Please give the two enclosed letters to my
mother, and have patience, I pray, till God brings
me home, when I will honourably repay you. My
greetings to Stephen Pirkheimer and other good
friends, and let me know if any of your loves
are dead. Read this according to the sense: I am
hurried.

Given in Venice, the Sunday before Whitsunday, the year 1506.

Albrecht Dürer.

Tomorrow it is good to confess.

IV

8th March, 1506

FIRST my willing service to you, dear Herr
Pirkheimer. I send you herewith a ring with
a sapphire about which you wrote so ur-

9

gently. I could not send it sooner, for the past
two days I have been running around to all the
German and Italian goldsmiths that are in all
Venice with a good assistant whom I hired; and
we made comparisons, but were unable to match
this one at the price, and only after much en-
treaty could I get it for 18 ducats 4 marcelli from
a man who was wearing it on his own hand and
who let me have it as a favour, as I gave him
to understand that I wanted it for myself. And
as soon as I had bought it a German goldsmith
wanted to give me 3 ducats more for it than
I paid, so I hope that you will like it. Everybody
says that it is a good stone, and that in Germany it would be worth about 50 florins; however, you will know whether they tell truth or
lies. I understand nothing about it. I had first of
all bought an amethyst for 12 ducats from a man
whom I thought was a good friend, but he de-
ceived me, for it was not worth 7; but the matter was arranged between us by some good fellows; I will give him back the stone and make
him a present of a dish of fish. I was glad to do
so and took my money back quickly. As my good
friend values the ring, the stone is not worth
much more than 10 Rhenish florins, whilst the
gold of the ring weighs about up to 5 florins,
so that I have not gone beyond the limit set
me, as you wrote "from 15 to 20 florins." But the
other stone I have not yet been able to buy, for

one finds them rarely in pairs; but I will do all I can about it. They say here that such trumpery fool's work is to be had cheaper in Germany, especially now at the Frankfurt Fair. For the Italians take such stuff abroad. And they laugh at me, especially about the jacinth cross, when I speak of 2 ducats, so write quickly and tell me what I am to do. I have heard of a good diamond ornament in a certain place, but I do not yet know what it will cost. I shall buy it for you until you write again, for emeralds are as dear as anything I have seen in all my days. It is easy enough for anyone to get a small amethyst if he thinks it worth 20 or 25 ducats.

It really seems to me you must have taken a mistress; only beware you don't get a master. But you are wise enough about your own affairs.

Dear Pirkheimer, Andreas Künhofer sends you his service. He intends in the meantime to write to you, and he prays you if necessary to explain for him to the Council why he does not stay at Padua; he says there is nothing there for him to learn. Don't be angry I pray you with me for not sending all the stones on this occasion, for I could not get them all ready. My friends tell me that you should have the stone set with a new foil and it will look twice as good again, for the ring is old, and the foil spoiled. And I beg you too to tell my mother to write me soon and have good care of herself. Herewith I commend myself to you.

11

Given at Venice on the second Sunday in Lent.
1506.

Albrecht Dürer.

Greetings to your loves.

V

2nd April, 1506

FIRST my willing service to you, dear Sir.
I received a letter from you on the Thursday before Palm Sunday, together with the
emerald ring, and went immediately to the man
from whom I got the rings. He will give me back
my money for it, although it is a thing that he does
not like to do; however, he has given me his word
and he must hold to that. Do you know that the
jewellers buy emeralds abroad and sell them
here at a profit? But my friends tell me that the
other two rings are well worth 6 ducats apiece,
for they say that they are fine and clear and contain no flaws. And they say that instead of taking
them to the valuer you should enquire for such
rings as they can show you and then compare
them and see whether they are like them; and if
when I got them by exchange I had been willing
to lose 2 ducats on the three rings, Bernard Holzbeck, who was present at the transaction, would
have bought them of me. I have since sent you

a sapphire ring by Franz Imhof, I hope it has reached you. I think I made a good bargain at that place, for they offered to buy it of me at a profit on the spot. But I shall find out from you, for you know that I understand nothing about such things and am forced to trust those who advise me.

The painters here you must know are very un-friendly to me. They have summoned me three times before the magistrates, and I have had to pay 4 florins to their School. You must know too that I might have gained much money if I had not undertaken to make the painting for the Germans, for there is a great deal of work in it and I cannot well finish it before Whitsuntide; yet they only pay me 85 ducats for it. That, you know, will go in living expenses, and then I have bought some things, and have sent some money away, so that I have not much in hand now; but I have made up my mind not to leave here until God enables me to repay you with thanks and to have 100 florins over besides. I should easily earn this if I had not got to do the German pic-ture, for, except the painters, everyone wishes me well.

Please tell my mother to speak to Wolgemut about my brother, and to ask him whether he can give him work until I get back, or whether he can find employment with others. I should like to have brought him with me to Venice, which would have been useful both to me and to him and he would have learned the language, but she was afraid that the sky would fall on him. I pray you keep an eye on him: women are no use for that. Tell the boy, as you can so well, to be studious and independent till I come, and not to rely on his mother, for I cannot do everything although I shall do my best. If it were only for myself, I should not starve; but to provide for so many is too hard for me, and nobody is throwing money away.

Now I commend myself to you, and tell my mother to be ready to sell at the Crown Fair. I am expecting my wife to come home, and have written to her too about everything. I shall not purchase the diamond ornament until you write. I do not think I shall be able to return home before next Autumn. What I earn for the picture which was to have been ready by Whitsuntide will all be gone in living expenses and payments. But what I gain afterwards I hope to save. If you think it right, say nothing of this and I shall keep putting it off from day to day and writing as though I was just coming. Indeed I am quite irresolute; I do not know myself what I shall do. Write to me again soon.

Given on Thursday before Palm Sunday in the year 1506.

Albrecht Dürer.

Your servant.

25th April, 1506

FIRST my willing service to you, dear Sir. I wonder why you do not write to me to say how you like the sapphire ring which Hans Imhof has sent you by the messenger Schön from Augsburg. I do not know whether it has reached you or not. I have been to Hans Imhof and enquired, and he says that he knows no reason why it should not have reached you, and there is a letter with it which I wrote to you, and the stone is done up in a sealed packet and has the same size as is drawn here, for I drew it in my notebook. I managed to get it only after hard bargaining. The stone is clear and fine, and my friends say it is very good for the money I gave for it. It weighs about 5 florins Rhenish, and I gave for it 18 ducats and 4 marzelle, and if it should be lost I should be half mad, for it has been valued at quite twice what I gave for it. There were people who would have given me more for it the moment I had bought it. So, dear Herr Pirkheimer, tell Hans Imhof to enquire of the messenger what he has done with the letter and packet. The messenger was sent off by Hans Imhof the younger on the 11th March.

Now may God keep you, and let me commend my mother to you. Tell her to take my brother to Wolgemut that he may work and not be idle.

Ever your servant.

Read by the sense. I am in a hurry, for I have
seven letters to write, – part written. I am sorry
for Herr Lorenz. Greet him and Stephen Paumgartner.

  Given at Venice in the year 1506, on St. Mark's
Day. Write me an answer soon, for I shall have
no rest till I hear. Andreas Künhofer is deadly ill
as I have just heard.

Albrecht Dürer.

VII

28th August, 1506

TO the first greatest man in the world; your
servant and slave, Alberto Dürer, sends salu-
tation to his magnificent Master Wilibaldo
Pirkamer. By my faith, I hear gladly and with
great pleasure of your health and great honour,
and I marvel how it is possible for a man like
you to stand against so many, tyrants, bullies,
and soldiers. Not otherwise than by the grace of
God. When I read your letter about this strange
abuse it gave me great fright; I thought it was
a serious matter. But I warrant you frighten even
Schott's men, for you look wild enough, especially on holy days with your skipping gait! But
it is very improper for such a soldier to smear
himself with civet. You want to be a regular silk
tail, and you think that if only you manage to

please the girls, it is all right. If you were only as
taking a fellow as I am, I should not be so pro-
voked. You have so many loves that it would
take you a month and more to visit each.

However, let me thank you for having arranged
my affairs so satisfactorily with my wife. I know
there is no lack of wisdom in you. If only you
were as gentle as I am, you would have all the
virtues. Thank you, too, for everything you are
doing for me, if only you would not bother me
about the rings. If they do not please you, break
off their heads and throw them in the privy, as
Peter Weisweber says. What do you mean by
setting me to such dirty work, I have become
a gentiluomo at Venice. I have heard that you
can make lovely rhymes; you would be a find
for our fiddlers here. They play so beautifully
that they weep over their own music. Would
God that our Rechenmeister girl could hear them,
she would cry too. At your command I will again
lay aside my anger and behave even better than
usual.

But I cannot get away from here in two months,
for I have not enough money yet to start myself off, as I have written to you before; and so I
pray you if my mother comes to you for a loan,
let her have 10 florins till God helps me out. Then
I will scrupulously repay you the whole.

With this I am sending you the glass things by
the messenger. And as for the two carpets, An-

thon Kolb will help me to buy the most beautiful,
the broadest, and the cheapest. As soon as I have
them I will give them to Imhof the younger to
pack off to you. I shall also look after the crane's
feathers. I have not been able to find any as yet.
But of swan's feathers for writing with there are
plenty. How would it do if you stuck them on
your hats in the meantime?

A book printer of whom I enquired tells me
that he knows of no Greek books that have been
brought out recently, but any that he comes
across he will acquaint me with that I may write
to you about them. And please inform me what
sort of paper you want me to buy, for I know of
no finer quality than we get at home. As to the
Historical pieces, I see nothing extraordinary in
what the Italians make that would be specially
useful for your work. It is always the same thing.
You yourself know more than they paint. I have
sent you a letter recently by the messenger Kannengiesser. Also I should like to know how you
are managing with Kunz Imhof.

Herewith let me commend myself to you. Give
my willing service to our prior. Tell him to pray
God for me that I may be protected, and especially from the French sickness, for there is nothing I fear more now and nearly everyone has it.
Many men are quite eaten up and die of it. And
greet Stephen Paumgartner and Herr Lorenz and
those who kindly ask after me.

Given at Venice on the 18th August, 1506.

Albrecht Dürer.

Noricus civis

P.S. Lest I forget, Andreas is here and sends you his service. He is not yet strong, and is in want of money. His long illness and debts have eaten up everything he had. I have myself lent him 8 ducats, but don't tell anyone, in case it should come back to him. He might think I told you in bad faith. You must know, too, that he behaves himself so honourably that everyone wishes him well. I have a mind, if the King comes to Italy, to go with him to Rome.

VIII

8th September, 1506

MOST learned, approved, wise, master of many languages, keen to detect all uttered lies, and quick to recognize real truth, honourable, Herr Wilibald Pirkheimer, your humble servant, Albrecht Dürer, wishes you all health, great and worthy honour, with the devil as much of such nonsense as you like.

I will wager that for this you too would think me an orator of a hundred headings. A chamber must have more than four corners which is

to contain gods of memory. I will not addle my
pate with it. I will recommend it to you, but I
believe that however many chambers there may
be in the head, you would have a little bit in each
of them. The Margrave would not grant a long
enough audience. A hundred headings and to
each head say a hundred words: that takes 9 days,
7 hours, 52 minutes, not counting the sighs, which
I have not yet reckoned; but you could not get
through the whole in one go: it would draw itself
out like some dotard's speech.

I have taken every trouble about the carpets,
but I cannot find any wide ones; they are all narrow and long. However, I still look out for them
every day, and so does Anthon Kolb. I gave your
respects to Bernhard Hirschvogel and he sent
you his service. He is full of sorrow for the death
of his son, the nicest boy that I have ever seen.
I can't get any of your fool's feathers. Oh, if you
were only here, how you would admire these
fine Italian soldiers! How often I think of you!
Would God that you and Kuntz Kamerer could
see them! They have scythe-shaped lances with
218 points; if they only touch a man with them
he dies, for they are all poisoned. Heigho! but I
can do it well, I'll be an Italian soldier. The Venetians are collecting many men; so is the Pope
and the King of France. What will come of it I
don't know, for people scoff at our King a great
deal.

Wish Stephen Paumgartner much happiness from me. I can't wonder at his having taken a wife. My greeting to Borsch, Herr Lorenz, and our fair friend, as well as to your Rechenmeister girl, and thank your Club for its greeting; says it 's a dirty one. I sent you olive-wood from Venice to Augsburg, where I let it stay, a full ten hundred weight. But it says it won't wait, hence the stink.

My picture, you must know, says it would give a ducat for you to see it. It is well paint- ed and finely coloured. I have got much praise but little profit by it. I could have easily earned 200 ducats in the time, and I have had to decline big commissions in order to come home. I have shut up all the painters, who used to say that I was good at engraving, but that in painting I didn't know how to handle my colours. Now they all say they never saw better colouring.

My French mantle greets you, and so does my Italian coat. It seems to me that you smell of gallantry. I can scent it from here; and they say here, that when you go courting, you pretend to be no more than 25 years old. – Oh, yes! multiply that and I 'll believe it. My friend, there 's a devil of a lot of Italians here who are just like you. I don't know how it is!

The Doge and the Patriarch have seen my picture. Herewith let me commend myself as your

servant. I really must sleep, for it's striking seven
at night, and I have already written to the Prior
of the Augustines, to my father-in-law, to Mistress
Dietrich, and to my wife, and they are all sheets
cram full. So I have had to hurry over this. Read
according to the sense. You would do it better
if you were writing to princes. Many good nights
to you, and days too. Given at Venice on Our
Lady's Day in September.

You need n't lend my wife and mother anything. They have got money enough.

Albert Dürer.

IX

23 Sept. 1506

YOUR letter telling me of the overflow-
ing praise that you received from princes
and nobles gave me great allegrezza. You
must have changed completely to have become
so gentle; I must do likewise when I meet you
again. Know also that my picture is finished, likewise another quadro, the like of which I never
made before. And as you are so pleased with
yourself, let me tell you now that there is no
better Madonna picture in all the land, for all
the painters praise it as the nobles do you. They
say that they have never seen a nobler, more
charming painting.

*The **Madonna** with Greenfinch. 1506. Oil on wood.*

The Feast of the Rose Garlands. 1506. Oil on wood. (Dürer spent close to eight months of his stay in Venice on this painting. It brought him fame but little money.)

The oil for which you wrote I am sending by Kannengiesser. And burnt glass that I sent you from by Färber—tell me if it reached you safely. As Venice for the carpets, I have not bought any yet, for I cannot find any square ones. They are all narrow and long. If you would like any of these, I will willingly buy them; let me know about it.

Know also that in four weeks at the latest I shall be finished here, for I have to paint first some portraits that I have promised, and in order that I may get home soon, I have refused, since my picture was finished, orders for more than 2000 ducats; all my neighbours know of this.

Now let me commend myself to you. I had much more to write, but the messenger is ready to start; besides, I hope, if God will, to be with you again soon and to learn new wisdom from you. Bernhard Holzbeck told me great things of you, but I believe that he did so because you have become his brother-in-law. But nothing makes me more angry than to hear anyone say that you are handsome, for then I should have to be ugly; that would make me mad. The other day I found a grey hair on my head, which was produced by sheer misery and annoyance. I think I am fated to have evil days.

My French mantle and the doublet and the brown coat send you a hearty greeting. But I should like to see what your drinking club can do that you hold yourself so high.

Given the year 1506 on Wednesday after St.
Matthew's.

Albrecht Dürer.

X

About the 13th October, 1506

SINCE I know that you are aware of my devotion to your service, there is no need to
write about it; but so much the more necessary is it for me to tell you of the great delight
it gives me to hear of the high honour and fame
that you have attained to by your manly wisdom and learned skill. This is the more to be
wondered at, for seldom or never can the like be
found in a young body; but it comes to you by
the special grace of God, as it does to me. How
pleased we both feel when we think well of
ourselves, I with my picture, and you con vostra learning! When anyone praises us we hold
up our head and believe him, yet perhaps he is
only some false flatterer who is making fun of us,
so don't credit anyone who praises you, for you
have no notion how unmannerly you are.

I can readily portray you to myself standing before the Margrave and making pretty speeches.
You carry on just as though you were making
love to the Rosentaler girl, cringing so.

It did not escape me, when you wrote the last letter, you were full of amorous thoughts. You ought to be ashamed of yourself, for making yourself out so good looking when you are so old. Your flirting is like a big shaggy dog playing with a little kitten. If you were only as nice and sleek as I am, I might understand it; but when I get to be a burgomaster I will shame you with the Luginsland, as you do the pious Zamener and me. I will have you shut up there for once with the Rechenmeister, Rosentaler, Gärtner, Schütz, and Por girls, and many others whom for shortness I will not name. They must deal with you.

They ask after me more than after you, however, for you yourself write that both girls and ladies ask after me—that is a sign of my virtue! But if God brings me home again safely, I do not know how I shall get along with you with your great wisdom; but I 'm glad on account of your virtue and good nature; and your dogs will be the better for it, for you will not beat them lame any more. But if you are so highly respected at home, you will not dare to be seen speaking with a poor painter in the streets, it would be a great disgrace, con poltrone di pintore.

Oh, dear Herr Pirkheimer, this very minute, while I was writing to you in good humour, the fire alarm sounded and six houses over by Peter Pender's are burned, and woollen cloth of mine, for which I paid only yesterday 8 ducats, is burned; so I too am in trouble. There are often fire alarms here.

As for your plea that I should come home quickly, I will come just as soon as I can; but I must first gain money for my expenses. I have paid out about 100 ducats for colours and other things, and I have ordered two carpets which I shall pay for to-morrow; but I could not get them cheap. I will pack them up with my linen. Und da Ihr schreibt ich solle bald kommen oder Ihr wollt mirs Weib Klystieren, so ist Euch das nicht erlaubt, Ihr rittet sie denn zu Tode.*

Know, too, that I decided to learn dancing and went twice to the school, for which I had to pay the master a ducat. No one could get me to go there again. To learn dancing, I should have had to pay away all that I have earned, and at the end I should have known nothing about it. As for the glass, the messenger Färber will bring it to you. I cannot find out anywhere that they are printing any new Greek books. I will pack up a ream of your paper for you. I thought Keppler had more like it; but I have not been able to get the feathers you wanted, and so I bought white ones instead. If I find the green ones, I will buy some and bring them with me.

Stephen Paumgartner has written to me to buy him fifty Carnelian beads for a rosary. I have ordered them, but they are dear. I could not get

26

***"As for your writing that I should come soon or else you intend to give my wife an 'enema,' you're not allowed to do so, because you would ride her to death."**

any larger ones, and shall send them to him by the next messenger.

As to your question as to when I shall come home, I tell you, so that my lords may make their arrangements, that I shall have finished here in ten days. After that I should like to travel to Bologna to learn the secrets of the art of perspective, which a man there is willing to teach me. I should stay there about eight or ten days and then come back to Venice; after that I should come with the next messenger. How I shall freeze after this sun! Here I am a gentleman, at home a parasite. Let me know how old Dame Kormer behaves as a bride, and that you will not grudge her to me. There are many things about which I should like to write to you, but I shall soon be with you.

Given at Venice about the 14th day after Michaelmas, 1506.

Albrecht Dürer.

P.S. When will you let me know whether any of your children have died? You also wrote me once that Joseph Rummel had married ————'s daughter, and forgot to mention whose. How should I know what you mean? If I only had my cloth back! I am afraid my mantle has been burned too. That would drive me crazy. I seem doomed to bad luck; not more than three weeks ago a man ran away who owed me 8 ducats.

DIARY OF A JOURNEY IN
THE NETHERLANDS

1520—1521

Agnes Dürer, the artist's wife, in Netherlandish costume. Antwerp, 1521. Brown metallic point on paper with dark-violet ground.

DIARY OF A JOURNEY IN
THE NETHERLANDS

July, 1520 – July, 1521

* *
*

Anno 1520

ON Thursday after St. Kilian's Day, I, Albrecht Dürer, at my own charges and costs, took myself and my wife from Nuremberg away to the Netherlands, and the same day, after we had passed through Erlangen, we put up for the night at Baiersdorff, and spent there 3 crowns, less 6 pfennigs. From thence on the next day, Friday, we came to Forchheim, and there paid for the conveying thence on the journey to Bamberg 22 pf., and presented to the Bishop a painted Virgin and a "Life of the Virgin," an "Apocalypse," and a florin's worth of engravings. He invited me to be his guest, gave me a toll-pass and three letters of introduction, and settled my bill at the inn, where I had spent about a florin. I paid 6 florins in gold to the boatmen who took me from Bamberg to Frankfurt. Master Lucas Benedict and Hans the painter sent me a present of wine. Spent 4 pf. for bread and 13 pf. as tips.

Then I journeyed from Bamberg to Eltman, and showed my pass, and they let me go free. And

from there we passed by Zeil; in the meantime
I spent 21 pf. Next I came to Hassfurt, and showed
my pass, and they let me go without paying duty;
I paid 1 florin to the Bishop of Bamberg's chan-
cery. Next I came to Theres to the monastery,
and I showed my pass, and they also let me go
free; then we journeyed to Lower Euerheim.
There I stayed the night and spent 1 pf. Thence we
went to Meinberg, and I showed my papers and
was allowed to pass. Then we came to Schwein-
furt, where Dr. George Rebart invited me, and he
gave us wine in the boat: they let me also pass
free. 10 pf. for a roast fowl, 18 pf. in the kitchen
and to the boy. Then we travelled to Volkach and
I showed my pass, and we went on and came to
Schwarzach, and there we stopped the night and
spent 22 pf., and on Monday we were up early
and went toward Tettelbach and came to Kit-
zingen, and I showed my letter, and they let me
go on, and I spent 37 pf. After that we went past
Sulzfeld to Marktbreit, and I showed my letter and
they let me through, and we travelled by Frick-
enhausen to Ochsenfurth, where I showed my pass
and they let me go free; and we came to Eibel-
stadt, and from that to Haidingsfeldt, and thence
to Würzburg; there I showed my pass and they
let me go free. Thence we journeyed to Erla-
brunn and stopped the night there, and I spent
22 pf. From that we journeyed on past Retz-
bach and Zellingen and came to Karlstadt; here

I showed my pass and they let me go on. Thence I travelled to Gmunden, and there we break-fasted and spent 22 pf. I also showed my pass, and they let me go free. We travelled thence to Hofstetten; I showed my pass, and they let me through. We came next to Lohr, where I showed my pass and passed on; from there we came to Neustadt and showed our letter, and they let us travel on; also I paid 10 pf. for wine and crabs. From there we came to Rothenfels, and I showed my pass, and they let me go free, and we stayed there for a night, and spent 20 pf.; and on Wednesday early we started and passed by St. Eucharius and came to Heidenfeld, and thence to Triefenstein; from there we came to Homburg, where I showed my pass and they let me through; from there we came to Wertheim, and I showed my letter, and they let me go free, and I spent 57 pf. From there we went to Prozelten; here I showed my pass, and they let me through. Next we went on past Freudenberg, where I showed my letter once more, and they let me through; from there we came to Miltenberg and stayed there over night, and I also showed my pass and they let me go, and I spent 61 pf.; from there we came to Klingenberg. I showed my pass and they let me through; and we came to Wörth and from there passed Obernburg to Aschaffenburg; here I presented my pass and they let me through, and I spent 52 pf.; from there we journeyed on

33

to Selgenstadt; from there to Steinheim, where I showed my letter and they let me go on, and we stayed with Johannes for the night, who showed us the town and was very friendly to us; there I spent 16 pf., and so early on Friday morning we travelled to Kesselstadt, where I showed my pass and they let me go on; from there we came to Frankfurt, and I showed my pass again, and they let me through, and I spent 6 white pf. and one thaler and a half, and I gave the boy 2 white pf. Herr Jacob Heller gave me some wine at the inn.

I bargained to be taken with my goods from Frankfurt to Mainz for 1 florin and 2 white pf., and I also gave the lad 5 Frankfurt thaler, and for the night we spent 8 white pf. On Sunday I travelled by the early boat from Frankfurt to Mainz, and midway there we came to Höchst, where I showed my pass and they let me go on; I spent 8 Frankfurt pf. there. From there we journeyed to Mainz; I have also paid 1 white pf. for landing my things, besides 14 Frankfurt thaler to the boatmen and 18 pf. for a girdle; and I took passage in the Cologne boat for myself and my things for 3 florins, and at Mainz also I spent 17 white pf. Peter Goldschmidt, the warden there, gave me two bottles of wine. Veit Varnbüler invited me, but his host would take no payment from him, insisting on being my host himself; they showed me much honour.

So I started from Mainz, where the Main flows into the Rhine, and it was the Monday after Mary Magdalen's Day, and I paid 10 thaler for meat and bread, and for eggs and pears 9 thaler. Here, too, Leonhard Goldschmidt gave me wine and fowls in the boat to cook on the way to Cologne. Master Jobst's brother likewise gave me a bottle of wine, and the painters gave me two bottles of wine in the boat. From there we came to Elfeld, where I showed my letter and they took no toll; from there we came to Rudesheim and I gave 2 white pf. for loading the boat; then we came to Ehrenfels, and there I showed my letter, but I had to give two gold florins; if, however, I were to bring them a free pass within two months, the customs officer would give me back the 2 gold florins. From there we came to Bacharach, and there I had to promise in writing that I would either bring them a free pass in two months, or pay the toll; from there we came to Caub, and there again I showed my pass, but it would carry me no further, and I had to promise in writing as before; there I spent 11 thaler. Next we came to St. Goar, and here I showed my pass, and the customs officer asked me how they had treated me elsewhere, so I said I would pay him nothing; I gave 2 white pf. to the messenger. From there we came to Boppard, and I showed my pass to the Trier custom-house officer, and they let me go through, only I had to certify in writing under

35

my seal that I carried no common merchandise, and then the man let me go willingly. From there we came to Lahnstein, and I showed my pass, and the customs officer let me go through, but he asked me that I should speak for him to my most gracious Lord of Mainz, and he gave me a can of wine, too, for he knew my wife well and he was glad to see me. From there we came to Engers, which is in the Trier territory; I presented my pass and they let me go through; I said, too, that I would mention it to my Lord of Bamberg. From there we came to Andernach, and I showed my pass, and they let me go through; and I spent there 7 thaler and 4 thaler more; then on St. James's Day early I travelled from Andernach to Linz; from there we went to the custom house at Bonn, and there again they let me go through; from there we came to Cologne, and in the boat I spent 9 white pf. and 1 more, and 4 pf. for fruit. At Cologne I spent 7 white pf. for unloading, to the boatmen 14 thaler, and to Nicolas, my cousin, I made a present of my black fur-lined coat edged with velvet, and to his wife I gave a florin; also at Cologne Fugger gave me wine; Johann Grosserpecker also gave me wine, and my cousin Nicolas gave me wine. They gave us also a collation at the Barefoot Convent, and one of the monks gave me a handkerchief; moreover, Herr Johann Grosserpecker has given me 12 measures of the best wine, and I paid 2 white

36

*Woman in Netherlandish Costume. 1521. Brush drawing on paper
with dark-violet ground; white highlights.*

Girl of Cologne in Regional Dress; Agnes Dürer. 1521. Silverpoint.

pf. and 8 thaler to the boy; I have spent besides at Cologne 2 florins and 14 white pf. and 10 white pf. for packing, and 3 pf. for fruit; further, I gave 1 pf. at leaving, and 1 white pf. to the messenger.

From there we journeyed on St. Pantaleon's Day from Cologne to a village called Büsdorf. We lay there over night, and spent 3 white pf.; and early on Sunday, we travelled to Rödingen, where we had breakfast and spent 2 white pf. and 3 pf. more, and again 3 pf. Thence we came to Frei-Aldenhoven, where we lay the night, and spent 3 white pf.; thence we travelled early on Monday to Frelenberg, and passed the little town of Gangelt, breakfasting at a village called Süsterseel, and spent 2 white pf. 2 thaler, further 1 white pf., and again 2 white pf. From there we journeyed to Sittard, a pretty little town, and from there to Stocken, which belongs to Liège; where we had a fine inn and stayed there over night, and spent 4 white pf. And when we had crossed over the Maas we started off early on Tuesday morning and came to Merten Lewbehen [sic]: there we had breakfast and spent 2 stivers and gave a white pf. for a young fowl. From there we travelled across the heath and came to Stosser, where we spent 2 stivers, and lay there the night; from thence on Wednesday morning early we travelled to West-Meerbeck, where I paid 3 stivers for bread and wine; and we went on as far as Branthoek, where we had breakfast and spent

1 stiver; from there we travelled to Uylenberg, where we stayed the night and spent 3 stivers, 2 pf.; from there we travelled on Thursday early to op ten Kouys, where we breakfasted and spent 2 stivers; thence we came to Antwerp.

There I sent to Jobst Planckfelt's inn, and the same evening the Fugger's factor, by name Bernhard Stecher, invited me and gave us a costly meal—my wife dined at the inn. I paid the driver for bringing us three, 3 florins in gold, and 2 stivers—for carrying the goods.

On Saturday after the Feast of St. Peter in Chains, my host took me to see the burgomaster's house at Antwerp, which is newly built and large beyond measure, very well arranged with extraordinarily beautiful large rooms; a tower, splendidly ornamented; a very large garden; in short, such a noble house as I have never seen in all German lands. A very long new street has been built in his honour, and with his assistance, leading up to the house on both sides. I gave 3 stivers to the messenger, and 2 pf. for bread and 2 pf. for ink; and on Sunday, which was St. Oswald's Day, the Painters invited me to their hall with my wife and maid, where everything was of silver, and they had other costly ornaments and very costly meats; and all their wives were there too; and as I was being led to the table, everyone on both sides stood up as if they were leading some great lord. There were among them men of high position, who all showed me the greatest respect and bowed low to me, and said they would do everything in their power to serve and please me. And as I sat there in honour, there came the messenger of the Town Council of Antwerp with two servants and presented to me four cans of wine from the Magistrates of Antwerp, who told him to say that they wished thereby to show their respect for me and to assure me of their good-will; wherefore I returned them my humble thanks and offered my humble services. Thereupon came Master Peter, the town carpenter, and gave me two cans of wine with offer of his willing service; so when we had spent a long time together merrily, till late into the night, they accompanied us home with lanterns in great honour. They begged me to be assured of their good-will, and promised that in whatever I did they would help me in every way; so I thanked them, and laid down to sleep.

Also I have been in Master Quentin's house, and I have been in all the three great shooting places. I had a very splendid dinner at Staiber's. Another time at the Portuguese factor's, whose portrait I have drawn in charcoal; I have made a portrait of my host as well; Jobst Plankfelt gave me a branch of white coral; paid 2 stivers for butter and 2 stivers to the joiner at the Painters' armoury.

Also my host took me to the Painters' workshop

in the armoury at Antwerp, where they are mak- ing the triumphal arches through which King Charles is to make his entry. It is 400 bows in length and each arch is 40 feet wide; they are to be set up on both sides of the streets, beautifully arranged and two stories high, and on them they are to act the plays; and this costs to make, 4000 florins for the joiners and painters, and the whole work is very magnificently done.

I have dined again with the Portuguese factor, and once with Alexander Imhof. Sebald Fischer bought of me at Antwerp sixteen "Small Pas- sions" for 4 florins, thirty-two of the large books for 8 florins, also six engraved "Passions" for 3 florins, also twenty half-sheets of all kinds taken together at 1 florin to the value of 3 florins, and again 5 1-4 florins' worth of quarter-sheets,–forty- five of all kinds at 1 florin, and eight miscellane- ous leaves at 1 florin; it is paid.

To my host I have sold a "Madonna" picture, painted on small canvas, for 2 florins Rhenish. I took once more the portrait of Felix the lute player. 1 stiver for pears and bread; 2 stivers to the surgeon-barber; besides I have given 14 sti- vers for three small panels, besides 4 stivers for laying in the white and preparing them. I have dined once with Alexander the goldsmith, and once with Felix Hungersberg; once Master Joa- chim has eaten with me, and his partner also once.

Captain Felix Hungersperg. Antwerp, 1520. Pen.

Hans Pfaffrot from Danzig. 1520. Pen.

I have made a drawing in half colours for
the Painters. I have taken 1 florin for expenses.
I made Peter Wolffgang a present of four new
little pieces. Master Joachim's partner has again
dined with me. I gave Master Joachim 1 florin's worth of prints for lending me his apprentice and colours, and I gave his apprentice 3
crowns' worth of prints. I have sent the four new
pieces to Alexander, the goldsmith. I made charcoal portraits of these Genoese by name: Tomasin Florianus Romanus, native of Lucca, and his
two brothers, named Vincentius and Gerhard,
all three Bombelli. I have dined with Tomasin so
often ||||||||||||. The treasurer also gave me
a "Child's Head" on linen and a weapon from
Calicut, and one of the light wood reeds. Tomasin Imhof has also given me a plaited hat of
elder pith.

I dined once more with the Portuguese; I also
gave one of Tomasin's brothers 3 florins' worth
of engravings. Herr Erasmus has given me a
small Spanish mantilla and three portraits of men.
Tomasin's brother gave me a pair of gloves for
3 florins' worth of engravings. I have once more
made the portrait of Tomasin's brother Vincentius; and I gave Master Augustus Lombard two
of the Imagines. Moreover, I made a portrait of
the crooked-nosed Italian named Opitius. Also
my wife and maid dined one day at Herr Tomasin's; that makes four meals.

Our Lady's Church at Antwerp is so vast that many masses may be sung there at one time without interfering one with another. The altars are richly endowed; the best musicians that can be had are employed; the Church has many devout services and much stonework, and in particular a beautiful tower. I also visited the rich Abbey of St. Michael, where are the finest galleries of stonework that I have ever seen, and a rich throne in the choir. But at Antwerp they spare no cost in such things, for they have plenty of money.

I have made a portrait of Herr Nicolas, an astronomer who lives with the King of England, and is very helpful and of great service to me in many matters. He is a German, a native of Munich. Also I have made the portrait of Tomasin's daughter, Maid Zutta by name. Hans Pfaffroth gave me a Philip's florin for taking his portrait in charcoal. I have dined once more with Tomasin. My host's brother-in-law entertained me and my wife once. I changed 2 light florins for 24 stivers for living expenses; and I gave 1 stiver for a tip to a man who let me see an altarpiece.

The Sunday after the Feast of the Assumption I saw the great procession of Our Lady's Church at Antwerp, where all the whole town was gathered together, with all the trades and professions, and each was dressed in his best according to his

rank; every guild and profession had its sign by
which it might be recognized. Between the com-
panies were carried great costly gold pole-can-
dlesticks and their long old Frankish silver trumpets; and there were many pipers and drummers
in the German fashion; all were loudly and noisily
blown and beaten. I saw the procession pass
along the street, spread far apart so that they
took up much space crossways, but close behind
one another: goldsmiths, painters, stonecutters,
broiderers, sculptors, joiners, carpenters, sailors,
fishermen, butchers, leather workers, cloth mak-
ers, bakers, tailors, shoemakers, and all kinds of
craftsmen and workmen who work for their live-
lihood. There were likewise shop-keepers and
merchants with their assistants of all sorts. After
them came the marksmen with their guns, bows,
and cross-bows; then the horsemen and foot soldiers; then came a large company of the town
guard; then a fine troop of very gallant men,
nobly and splendidly costumed. Before them,
however, went all the religious orders and the
members of some foundations, very devoutly,
in their respective groups. There was, too, in this
procession, a great troop of widows, who sup-
port themselves by their own labour and ob-
serve special rules, all dressed from head to foot
in white linen robes made expressly for the occasion, very sorrowful to behold. Among them
I saw some very stately persons, the Canons of

Our Lady's Church with all their clergy, schol-
ars, and treasures. Twenty persons bore the im-
age of the Virgin Mary and of the Lord Jesus,
adorned in the richest manner, to the honour of
the Lord God. The procession included many delightful things splendidly got up, for example,
many wagons were drawn along with stagings
of ships and other constructions. Then there came
the company of the Prophets in their order, and
scenes from the New Testament, such as the An-
nunciation, the Three Magi riding great camels,
and other strange beasts, very skilfully arranged,
and also how Our Lady fled into Egypt—very
conducive to devotion—and many other things
which for shortness I must leave out. Last of all
came a great dragon, which St. Margaret and her
maidens led by a girdle; she was extraordinarily
beautiful. Behind her followed a St. George with
his squire, a very fine cuirassier. There also rode
in the procession many pretty and richly dressed
boys and girls in the costumes of many lands
representing various saints. This procession from
beginning to end, where it passed our house,
lasted more than two hours; there were so many
things there that I could not write them in a
book, so I let it alone.

I visited Fugger's house in Antwerp, which is
newly built, with a wonderful tower, broad and
high, and with a beautiful garden, and I also saw
his fine stallions. Tomasin has given my wife

fourteen ells of good thick arras for a mantle Journey
and three and a half ells of half satin to line it. I in the
drew a design for a lady's forehead band for the Nether-
goldsmith. The Portuguese factor has given me lands
a present of wine in the inn, both Portuguese
and French. Signor Rodrigo of Portugal has given
me a small cask full of all sorts of sweetmeats,
amongst them a box of sugar candy, besides two
large dishes of barley sugar, marchpane, many
other kinds of sugar-work, and some sugar-canes
just as they grow; I gave his servant in return
1 florin as a tip. I have again changed for my
expenses a light florin for 12 stivers.

The pillars in the Convent of St. Michael of Antwerp are all made out of single blocks of a beautiful black touchstone. Herr Ægidius, King Charles's
warden, has taken for me from Antwerp the "St.
Jerome in the Cell," the "Melancholy," and three
new "Marys," the "Anthony" and the "Veronica" for the good sculptor, Master Conrad,
whose like I have not seen; he serves Lady
Margaret, the Emperor's daughter. Also I gave
Master Ægidius a "Eustace" and a "Nemesis." I
owe my host 7 florins, 20 stivers, 1 thaler—that is,
on Sunday before St. Bartholomew: for sitting-
room, bedroom, and bedding I am to pay him 11
florins a month. I came to a new agreement with
my host on the 20th August—on the Monday
before St. Bartholomew's—I am to eat with him
and pay 2 stivers for the meal, and extra for drink,

45

but my wife and the maid can cook and eat up here.

I gave the Portuguese factor a statuette of a child; besides that, I gave him an "Adam and Eve," a "Jerome in his Cell," a "Hercules," a "Eustace," a "Melancholy," and a "Nemesis;" then of the half-sheets, three new "Virgins," the "Veronica," the "Anthony," "The Nativity," and "The Crucifixion," also the best of the quarter-sheets, eight pieces, and then the three books of the "Life of the Virgin," "The Apocalypse," and the "Great Passion," also the "Little Passion" and the "Passion" on copper, all together, 5 florins' worth. The same quantity I gave to Signor Rodrigo, the other Portuguese. Rodrigo has given my wife a small green parrot.

VISIT TO BRUSSELS

ON the Sunday after St. Bartholomew's, I travelled with Herr Tomasin from Antwerp to Mechlin, where we lay for the night; there I invited Master Conrad and a painter with him to supper, and this Master Conrad is the good carver in Lady Margaret's service. From Mechlin we travelled through the small town of Vilvorde and came to Brussels on Monday at midday; I gave the messenger 3 stivers; I dined with my lords at Brussels; also once with Herr Bannisis,

and I gave him a "Passion" on copper. I gave the Margrave Hansen of Brussels the letter of recom-
mendation which my lord of Bamberg wrote
for me, and I made him a present of a "Passion"
engraved on copper for a remembrance. I have
also dined once more with my lords of Nuremberg. I saw in the town hall at Brussels, in the
golden chamber, four paintings which the great
Master Rogier did; and behind the King's palace
in Brussels, the fountains, labyrinth, zoölogical
garden. Anything more beautiful and pleasing
to me, more like a paradise, I have never seen.
Erasmus is the name of the little man who wrote
out my supplication at Jacob Bannisis' house.

At Brussels there is a very splendid town hall,
large and covered with beautiful stonework, with
a noble open tower. I have made a portrait of
Master Conrad of Brussels by candle-light; he is
my host. At the same time I drew Doctor Lam-
parter's son in charcoal, and also the hostess. Also
I have seen the things which they have brought
to the King out of the new land of gold: a sun
all of gold, a whole fathom broad, and a moon,
too, of silver, of the same size, also two rooms
full of armour, and the people there with all
manner of wondrous weapons, harness, darts,
wonderful shields, extraordinary clothing, beds,
and all kinds of wonderful things for human use,
much finer to look at than prodigies. These
things are all so precious that they are valued

47

at 100,000 gulden, and all the days of my life
I have seen nothing that reaches my heart so
much as these, for among them I have seen won-
derfully artistic things and have admired the sub-
tle ingenuity of men in foreign lands; indeed, I
don't know how to express what I there found.

I also saw many other beautiful things at Brussels, and especially a great fish bone there, as vast
as if it had been built up of square stones; it was
a fathom long, very thick, weighs up to 1 cwt.
(15 centner), and it has the form as is here drawn;
it stood behind on the fish's head.

I have also been in the Lord of Nassau's house,
which is so magnificently built and so beautifully decorated. I have again dined twice with my
lords. Lady Margaret sent after me to Brussels
and promised that she would speak in my behalf
to King Charles, and has shown herself quite ex-
ceptionally kind to me; I sent her my engraved
"Passion" and such another to her treasurer, Jan
Marnix by name, and I made his portrait in charcoal. I paid 2 stivers for a buffalo ring, and also
2 stivers for opening St. Luke's picture.

When I was in Herr von Nassau's house I saw
in the chapel the fine painting that Master Hugo
has made, and I also saw two large beautiful
halls, and all the treasures in various parts of
the house, and the large bed in which fifty men
can lie. And I also saw the great stone which
the storm cast down in the field close to Herr von

Nassau. This house lies high, and there is a most beautiful view at which one cannot but won- der. And I think that in all German lands there is not the like of it.

Master Bernhard, the painter, invited me to din- ner, and had prepared a meal so costly that I do not think 10 florins will pay for it. Three friends invited themselves to it to give me good com- pany, to wit, Lady Margaret's treasurer, whose portrait I made, and the King's steward, de Me- tenye, and the town treasurer, Van Busleyden; I gave him a "Passion" engraved on copper, and he gave me in return a black Spanish bag worth 3 florins. And I also gave a "Passion" engraved on copper to Erasmus of Rotterdam; likewise one to Erasmus, the secretary of Bannisis. The man at Antwerp who gave me the "Child's Head" is called Lorenz Sterk. I took the portrait in char- coal of Master Bernhard, Lady Margaret's painter. I have taken Erasmus of Rotterdam's portrait once more. I gave Lorenz Sterk a sitting "St. Jerome" and the "Melancholy," and I made a portrait of my hostess's godmother. Six people whose portraits I painted at Brussels gave me nothing. I paid 3 stivers for two buffalo horns and 1 stiver for two Eulenspiegels.

So then on the Sunday after St. Giles', I trav- elled with Herr Tomasin to Mechlin and took leave of Herr Hans Ebner, and he would take nothing for my expenses while I was with him

seven days; I paid 1 stiver on behalf of Hans
Geuder; I gave 1 stiver as a tip to the host's
servant; and at Mechlin I took supper with the
Lady Nieuwekerke; and early on Monday I travelled from Mechlin to Antwerp.

AT ANTWERP

September 3 to October 4, 1520

I BREAKFASTED with the Portuguese factor,
who gave me three porcelain dishes, and Rodrigo gave me some Calicut feathers. I spent 1
florin and paid my messenger 2 stivers. I bought
Susanna a mantle for 2 florins, 10 stivers. My wife
paid 4 florins Rhenish for a washtub, a bellows, a
basin, a pair of slippers, wood for cooking, stock-
ings, a cage for the parrot, 2 jugs, and for tips; she
spent, moreover, for eating, drinking, and various
necessaries, 21 stivers.

Now on Monday after St. Giles' I am back
again at Jobst Planckfelter's, and have dined
with him as many times as are drawn here—
||||||||||||||||||. I gave Nicolas, Tomasin's man,
1 stiver; I paid 5 stivers for the little frame, and
1 stiver more. My host gave me an Indian cocoa-
nut and an old Turkish whip; then I have dined
||||||||||||| more with Tomasin. The two lords of
Rogendorf have invited me; I have dined once
with them and made a large drawing of their coat

Erasmus of Rotterdam. 1520. Charcoal.

The Harbor of Antwerp at the Schelde Gate. 1520. Pen.

of arms on wood, for engraving. I gave away 1 stiver; my wife changed a florin for 24 stivers; I gave 2 stivers as a tip. I have dined once in Focker's house with the young Jacob Rehlinger, and I have also dined once more with him. My wife has changed a florin for 24 stivers for expenses. I gave to Wilhelm Hauenhut, the servant of my lord Duke Frederick, the Platzgraf, an engraved "Jerome," and the two new half-sheets, the "Mary" and the "Anthony." I gave Herr Jacob Bannisis a good painting of a "Veronica" face, a "Eustace," a "Melancholy," and a sitting "Jerome," a "St. Anthony," the two new "Marys," and the new "Peasants." And I have given his secretary, Erasmus, who wrote my supplication, a sitting "Jerome," a "Melancholy," an "Anthony," the two new "Marys," and the "Peasants," and I have given him also two small "Marys," and all together what I have given is worth 7 florins, and I have given Master Marc, the goldsmith, a "Passion" on copper, and he gave me 3 florins in payment; besides this I have received 3 florins, 20 stivers, for prints. To the glazier Hönigen, I have given four little engravings. I have dined with Herr Bannisis | | |. I paid 4 stivers for carbon and black chalk; I have given 1 florin, 8 stivers for wood, and spent 3 stivers more. I have dined with the lords of Nuremberg | | | | | | | | |. Master Dietrich, the glass painter, sent me the red colour which is found in the new bricks at Antwerp. I made

a charcoal portrait of Jacob von Lubeck; he gave
my wife a Philip's florin. I have again changed
a Philip's florin for expenses.

I presented to Lady Margaret a seated "Jerome"
engraved on copper. I sold a woodcut "Passion"
for 12 stivers, besides an "Adam and Eve" for 4
stivers. Felix, the captain and lute-player, bought
a whole set of copper-engravings and a woodcut "Passion" and an engraved "Passion," two
half-sheets and two quarter-sheets, for 8 gold
florins; so I gave him another set of engravings.
I have taken Herr Bannisis's portrait in charcoal.
Rodrigo gave me another parrot, and I gave his
boy 2 stivers for a tip. I gave Johann von den
Winckel, the trumpeter, a small woodcut "Passion," "St. Jerome in his Cell," and a "Melancholy."
I paid 6 stivers for a pair of gloves. I paid 5 stivers for a bamboo rod, and George Schlaudersbach gave me another which cost 6 stivers. I have
dined once with Wolff Haller, who is employed
by the Fuggers, when he had invited my lords
of Nuremberg. I have received for works of art
2 Philip's florins, 6 stivers. I have again dined once
with my wife; I gave 1 stiver to Hans Denes' boy
for a tip. I have taken 100 stivers for works of art.
I made a charcoal portrait of Master Jacob, Lord
Rogendorf's painter, and I have drawn for Lord
Rogendorf his arms on wood, for which he gave
me seven ells of velvet.

I dined once more with the Portuguese; I took

the portrait of Master John Prost of Bruges, and he gave me 1 florin; it was done in charcoal; 23 stivers for a fur coat of rabbit-skin. I sent Hans Schwarz 2 golden florins for my picture in a letter sent through the Antwerp Fuggers to Augsburg. I gave 31 stivers for a red woollen shirt. I dined once more with Rogendorf. I gave 2 stivers for the colour which is found in the bricks; and I paid 9 stivers for an ox horn. I made a charcoal portrait of a Spaniard. I have dined once with my wife. I gave 2 stivers for a dozen little pipes; I gave 3 stivers for two little maplewood bowls, two such Felix gave my wife, and Master Jacob, the painter from Lubeck, has given my wife another; dined once with Rogendorf.

I paid 1 stiver for the printed "Entry into Antwerp," showing how the King was received with a splendid triumph; the gates were beautifully decorated, and there were plays, much rejoicing, and beautiful maidens in tableaux vivants, whose like I have seldom seen. Changed 1 florin for expenses. I have seen the bones of the great giant at Antwerp; his leg above his knee is five and a half feet long, and beyond measure heavy; so were his shoulder blades – a single one is broader than a strong man's back – and his other limbs. The man was eighteen feet high, and reigned at Antwerp and did great wonders, as is set out in an old book which belongs to the town magistrates.

Raphael of Urbino's effects have been all dispersed after his death, but one of his disciples, Tommaso of Bologna by name, a good painter, desired to see me, so he came to me and gave me a gold ring, an antique with a well-cut stone worth 5 florins, but I have been already offered twice as much for it; in return I gave him my best engravings, worth 6 florins. I bought a piece of calico for 3 stivers, I gave the messenger 1 stiver, and spent 3 stivers in company.

I presented to Lady Margaret, the Emperor's sister, a whole set of all my works, and have drawn her two pictures on parchment with the greatest pains and care; all this I have put at 30 florins, and I have had to draw the design of the house for her physician, the doctor, according to which he intends to build one, and for drawing that I would not willingly take less than 10 florins. I have given the servant 1 stiver, and I paid 1 stiver for brick colour; I have given Herr Nicolas Ziegler a "Christ lying dead," worth 3 florins. To the Portuguese factor I gave a painting of a "Child's Head," worth 1 florin. I have given 10 stivers for a buffalo horn; I gave 1 gold florin for an elk's hoof. I have done Master Adrian's portrait in charcoal. I gave 2 stivers for the "Condemnation" and the "Dialogue," 3 stivers to the messenger; to Master Adrian I have given 2 florins' worth of works of art; bought a piece of red chalk for 1 stiver. I have done Herr Wolff von

Rogendorf in silverpoint. Gave away 3 stivers; did the portrait of a noble lady at Tomasin's house. I have given to Nicolas a "Jerome in the Cell," and two new "Marys." On Monday after St. Michael's Day, 1520, I gave to Tommaso of Bologna a whole set of prints to send for me to Rome to another painter, who will send me Raphael's work in return. I dined once with my wife; gave 3 stivers for the little tract. The Bolognese has painted my portrait, which he will take with him back to Rome. I bought an elk's foot for 20 stivers, besides I paid 2 gold florins, 4 stivers, for Herr Hans Ebner's little panel; dined out; changed a crown for expenses; dined out. Am taking 11 florins for my expenses to Aachen; have received 2 florins, 4 stivers, from Ebner; paid 9 stivers for wood; gave Meyding 20 stivers for sending my box.

I have taken the portrait of a lady of Bruges, who has given me 1 Philip's florin. I gave away 3 stivers as a tip; paid 2 stivers for fir cones and 1 for stone colour; paid 13 stivers to the furrier, 1 stiver for leather; bought two mussels for 2 stivers. In John Gabriel's house I have taken the portrait of an Italian lord, who gave me 2 gold florins. Bought a portmanteau for 2 florins, 4 stivers.

VISIT TO AACHEN

ON Thursday after St. Michael's Day, I journeyed from Antwerp to Aachen, and I took 1 gulden and 1 noble with me; and after passing through Maestricht we came to Gülpen, and from there to Aix on Sunday; there I have spent up till now, with the fare and all, 3 florins. At Aachen I saw the well-proportioned pillars with their good capitals of green and red porphyry and granite which Carolus [Charlemagne] had brought from Rome and set up there. These are made truly according to Vitruvius's writings. At Aachen I bought an ox horn for 1 gold florin. I have taken the portraits of Herr Hans Ebner and George Schlaudersbach, and Hans Ebner's a second time. I paid 2 stivers for a fine whetstone, also 5 stivers for a bath and drinking in company; changed 1 florin for expenses. I gave the town servant who took me up into the hall 2 white pf.; spent 5 white pf. with companions, drinking and bathing; I have lost 7 stivers at play with Herr Hans Ebner at the Mirror. I have made a charcoal portrait of the young Christopher Groland, also of my host, Peter von Enden. I spent 3 stivers in company, and gave the messenger 1 stiver. I have taken the portraits of Paul Topler and Martin Pfinzing in my sketch-book.

I have seen the arm of the Emperor Henry, the

Paul Topler and Martin Pfinzing. October 1520. Silverpoint.

The Cathedral at Aachen, Seen from the Coronation Hall. October 1520. Silverpoint.

shirt and girdle of Our Lady, and other holy relics.
I have sketched the Church of Our Lady with its
surroundings. I took Stürm's portrait. Made the
portrait in charcoal of Peter von Enden's brother-in-law. Have given 10 white pf. for a large
ox horn; gave 2 white pf. for a tip, and I have
changed 1 florin for expenses. I have lost 3 white
pf. at play, also 2 stivers; gave 2 white pf. to the
messenger. I have given Tomasin's daughter the
painted "Trinity," it is worth 4 florins; paid 1
stiver for washing. I took the portrait in charcoal of the Köpffingrin's sister at Aachen, and
another in silverpoint. Spent 3 white pf. for a
bath; paid 8 white pf. for a buffalo horn; 2 white
pf. for a girdle; paid 1 Philip's florin for a scarlet
shawl; 6 pf. for paper; changed 1 florin for expenses; paid 2 white pf. for washing.

On the 23rd day of October King Charles was
crowned at Aachen; there I saw all manner of
lordly splendour, the like of which those who
live in our parts have never seen—all, as it has
been described. I gave Mathes works of art worth
2 florins, and I presented Stephen, Lady Margaret's
chamberlain, with 3 prints. Paid 1 florin, 10 white
pf. for a cedarwood rosary; gave 1 stiver to little
Hans in the stable, and 1 stiver to the child in the
house; lost 2½ stivers at play; spent 2 stivers,
gave 2 stivers to the barber. I have again changed
1 florin; I gave away 7 white pf. in the house on
leaving.

SECOND VISIT TO COLOGNE

AND I travelled from Aachen to Jülich, and thence to . . . ; paid 4 stivers for two eyeglasses. I played away 2 stivers in an embossed silver medal of the king. I have given 8 white pf. for two ox horns.

On the Friday before St. Simon and St. Jude I left Aachen and travelled to Düren, where I visited the church where St. Anne's head is. Thence we travelled and came on Sunday, which was St. Simon and St. Jude's Day, to Cologne. I had lodging, food, and drink at Brussels with my lords of Nuremberg, and they would take nothing from me for it, and at Aachen likewise I ate with them three weeks and they brought me to Cologne, and would take nothing for it.

I have bought a tract of Luther's for 5 white pf., besides 1 white pf. for the "Condemnation of Luther," the pious man, besides 1 white pf. for a Paternoster, and 2 white pf. for a girdle, 1 white pf. for one pound of candles; changed 1 florin for expenses. I had to give Herr Leonhard Groland my great ox horn, and to Hans Ebner I had to give my large rosary of cedarwood. Paid 6 white pf. for a pair of shoes; I gave 2 white pf. for a little skull; 1 white pf. I gave for beer and bread; 1 white pf. for a "pertele" [? braid]. I have given 4 white pf. to two messengers; I have given 2 white pf. to Nicolas's daughter for lace, also 1 white pf. to a messenger. I gave prints worth 2 florins to Herr Ziegler Linhard; paid the barber 2 white pf.; paid 3 white pf. and then 2 white pf. for opening the picture which Master Stephan made at Co- logne; I gave the messenger 1 white pf., and spent 2 white pf. drinking in company. I made the portrait of Gottschalk's sister; I paid 1 white pf. for a little tract. At Cologne, on Sunday evening after All Saints' Day in the year 1520, I saw the nobles dance and banquet in the Emperor Charles's dancing saloon; it was splendidly arranged. I have drawn for Staiber his coat of arms on wood. I gave a "Melancholy" to a young count at Cologne, and a new "Mary" to Duke Frederick. I have made Nicolas Haller's portrait in charcoal; paid 2 white pf. to the door porter. I have given 3 white pf. for two little tracts, also 10 white pf. for a cow horn.

At Cologne I went to St. Ursula's Church and to her grave, and saw the holy maiden and the other great relics. Fernberger's portrait I took in charcoal; changed 1 florin for expenses. I gave Nicolas's wife 8 white pf. when she invited me as a guest. I bought two prints for 1 stiver. Herr Hans Ebner and Herr Nicolas Groland would take nothing from me for eight days at Brussels, three weeks at Aachen, and fourteen days at Cologne. I made the nun's portrait, and gave 7 white pf. to the nun. I made her a present of three half-sheet engravings on copper. My Confirmation from the

Emperor came to my lords of Nuremberg the
Monday after St. Martin's, the year 1520, after great
trouble and labour. I gave Nicolas's daughter 7
white pf. on departing, 1 florin to his wife, and
again 1 ort to his daughter on leaving; and I started
away from Cologne. Before that, Staiber invited
me once as his guest, and so did my cousin Nicolas once, and old Wolfgang once, and once besides I dined as his guest. I have given Nicolas's
man a "Eustace" on leaving, and his little daughter another ort, as they took much trouble for
me. I have given 1 florin for a little ivory skull,
and 1 white pf. for a turned box, also 7 white pf.
for a pair of shoes, and I gave Nicolas's man a
"Nemesis" on leaving.

SECOND JOURNEY
FROM COLOGNE TO ANTWERP

I STARTED off early by boat from Cologne on
Wednesday after St. Martin's, and went as far
as . . . Paid 6 white pf. for a pair of shoes. I
gave 4 white pf. to the messenger. From Cologne
I travelled by the Rhine to Zons, from Zons to
Neuss, and from thence to Stain where we
stayed the day, and I spent 6 white pf. Thence
we came to Düsseldorf, a little town, where I spent
2 white pf.; from thence to Kaiserswerth; from
thence to Duisburg, another little town, and we

passed two castles, Angerort and Rurort; thence we went to Orsoy, a little town; from thence we went to Rheinberg, another little town, where I lay over night, and spent 6 white pf.; from there I travelled to the following towns, Burg Wesel, Rees, and from there to Emmerich. We came next to Thomas, and from there to Nymwegen; there we stayed over the night and spent 4 white pf.; from Nymwegen I travelled to Tiel, and from there to Herzogenbusch. At Emmerich I stopped and spent 3 white pf. on a very good meal. There I took the portrait of a goldsmith's apprentice, Peter Federmacher of Antwerp, and of a woman. The reason of our staying was that a great storm of wind overtook us. I spent besides 5 white pf., and I changed 1 florin for expenses; also I took the host's portrait, and we did not get to Nymwegen until Sunday; I gave the boatmen 20 white pf. Nymwegen is a beautiful city, and has a fine church and a well-situated castle; from there we travelled to Tiel, where we left the Rhine and continued on the Maas to Heerewarden, where the two towers stand; there we lay over night, and during this day I spent 7 stivers. From there we started early on Tuesday for Bommel on the Maas; there a great storm of wind overtook us and we hired some peasant horses and rode without saddles as far as Herzogenbusch, and I paid 1 florin for the journey by boat and horse. Herzogenbusch is a beautiful city, and has an extremely beautiful church and a strong fortress; there I spent 10 stivers, although Arnold settled for the repast. The goldsmiths came to me and showed me great honour. From there we travelled on Our Lady's Day early and came through the large and beautiful village of Oosterwyck. We breakfasted at Tilborch and spent 4 white pf.; from there we came to Baarle, lay the night there, and spent 5 stivers, and my companions got into an argument with the innkeeper, so we went on in the night to Hoogstraten; there we stopped two hours and went by St. Leonhard Kirchen to Harscht. We breakfasted there and spent 4 stivers.

SECOND STAY AT ANTWERP

November 22 – December 3, 1520

FROM there we journeyed to Antwerp and gave the driver 15 stivers. This was on Thursday after Our Lady's Assumption [by error for Presentation]; and I gave an engraving of the "Passion" to John, Jobst Schwager's man, and I made a portrait of Nicolas Sopalis, and on the Thursday after Our Lady's Assumption [Presentation], 1520, I was once more back in Jobst Planckfelt's house; I have eaten with him |||| times. My wife–||–changed 1 florin for expenses, besides a crown; and the seven weeks that I have been away my wife and maid have spent 7 crowns and bought another 4 florins' worth of things. I spent 4 stivers in company. I have dined with Tomasin | | | | | | times. On St. Martin's Day my wife had her purse cut off in Our Lady's Church at Antwerp; there were 2 florins in it, and the purse itself, besides what was in it, was worth another florin, and some keys were in it, too. On the eve before St. Catherine's I paid Jobst Planckfelt, my host, 10 gold crowns for my reckoning. I dined two times with the Portuguese. Rodrigo gave me six Indian nuts, so I gave his boy 2 stivers for a tip. I paid 19 stivers for parchment; changed 2 crowns for expenses. I sold two "Adam and Eves," one "Sea Monster," one "Jerome," one "Knight," one "Nemesis," one "St. Eustace," one whole sheet, besides seventeen etched pieces, eight quarter-sheets, and ten woodcuts, seven of the bad woodcuts, two books, and ten small wood "Passions," the whole for 8 florins. Also I exchanged three large books for one ounce [ell of?] camlet. I changed a Philip's florin for expenses and my wife likewise changed a florin.

At Zierikzee in Zeeland a whale has been washed ashore by a great tide and storm; it is much more than a hundred fathoms long; no one in Zeeland has ever seen one even one-third as long, and the fish cannot get off the land. The people would be glad to see it gone, for they

fear the great stink, for it is so big they say it
could not be cut in pieces and the oil got out of
it in half a year.

Stephen Capello has given me a cedarwood
rosary, in return for which I was to take and have
taken his portrait. I paid 4 stivers for furnace
brown and a pair of snuffers; I gave 3 stivers for
paper; made a portrait of Felix, kneeling, in his
book in pen and ink, and Felix gave me one hundred oysters. I gave Herr Lazarus, the great man,
an engraved "Jerome" and three large books.
Rodrigo sent me some wine and oysters. I paid
7 white pf. for black chalk.

I have had to dinner Tomasin, Gerhard, Tomasin's daughter, her husband, the glass painter
Hennick, Jobst and his wife, and Felix, which cost
2 florins. Tomasin made me a gift of four ells
of grey damask for a doublet. I have changed a
Philip's florin for expenses.

VISIT TO ZEELAND

December 3 – 14, 1520

ON St. Barbara's Eve I travelled from Antwerp to Bergen-op-Zoom; I paid 2 stivers
for the horse, and I spent 1 florin 6 stivers
there. At Bergen I bought my wife a thin Netherlandish headcloth, which cost 1 florin, 7 stivers, besides 6 stivers for three pairs of shoes, 1 stiver for

View of Bergen-op-Zoom. December 1520. Silverpoint.

Young Woman from Bergen-op-Zoom; Old Woman, December 1520. Silverpoint

eyeglasses, and 6 stivers for an ivory button; gave 2 stivers for a tip. I have drawn the por- traits in charcoal of Jan de Has, his wife, and two daughters; and the maid and the old woman in silverpoint, in my sketch-book. I saw the Van Bergen house, which is a very large and beautiful building. Bergen is a pleasant place in summer, and two great fairs are held there yearly. On Our Lady's Eve I started with my companions for Zeeland, and Sebastian Imhof lent me five flor- ins; and the first night we lay at anchor in the sea; it was very cold and we had neither food nor drink. On Saturday we came to Goes, and there I drew a girl in the costume of the place. Thence we travelled to Arnemuiden, and I paid 15 stivers for expenses. We went by a sunken place, where we saw the tops of the roofs stand- ing up above the water, and we went by the is- land of Wolfersdyk, and passed the little town Kortgene on another island lying near. Zeeland has seven islands, and Arnemuiden, where I lay the night, is the biggest. From there I travelled to Middelburg. There in the abbey Jan de Ma- buse has made a great picture, not so good in the drawing as in the colouring. From there I went to the Veere, where ships from all lands lie. It is a very fine little town. But at Arnemuiden, where I landed, there happened to me a great misfortune. As we were coming to land and get- ting out our rope, just as we were getting on shore, a great ship ran into us so hard that in the crush I let everyone get out before me, so that no one but myself, George Kötzler, two old women, the sailor, and a little boy were left in the ship. When now the other ship knocked against us and I with those mentioned was on the ship and could not get out, the strong rope broke, and at the same moment a violent storm of wind arose which forcibly drove back our ship. So we all called for help, but no one would risk himself, and the wind carried us back out to sea. Then the skipper tore his hair and cried aloud, for all his men had landed and the ship was unmanned. It was a matter of fear and danger, for there was a great wind and no more than six persons in the ship, so I spoke to the skipper that he should take heart and have hope in God, and should take thought for what was to be done. He said that if he could pull up the small sail, he would try if we could come again to land. So we all helped one another and pulled it half-way up with difficulty, and went on again towards the land. And when those on the land who had already given us up saw how we helped ourselves, they too came to our aid, and we got to land.

Middelburg is a good town; it has a very beautiful town hall with a fine tower. There is much art shown in all things here. There are very rich and beautiful stalls in the abbey, and a splendid gallery of stone and a beautiful parish church.

The town is excellent for sketching. Zeeland is beautiful and wonderful to see on account of the water, for it stands higher than the land. I have made a portrait of my host at Arnemuiden. Master Hugo, Alexander Imhof, and the Hirschvogel's servant Frederick gave me each of them an Indian nut that they had won at play, and the host gave me a sprouting bulb. Early on Monday morning we went back to the ship and set out for the Veere and for Zierikzee; I wanted to get sight of the great fish, but the tide had carried it off again. I paid 2 florins for fare and expenses and 2 florins for a rug, 4 stivers for a fig-cheese and 3 stivers for carriage, and I lost 6 stivers at play. When we came back to Bergen I gave 10 stivers for an ivory comb.

I have taken Schnabhan's portrait, and I have also taken the portrait of my host's son-in-law, Klautz. Gave 2 florins less 5 stivers for a piece of tin; also 2 florins for a bad piece of tin. I have also taken the portrait of little Bernard of Brussels, George Kötzler, and the Frenchman from Kamrick; each of them gave me 1 florin at Bergen. Jan de Has' son-in-law gave me 1 Horn florin for his portrait, and Kerpen of Cologne also gave me a florin, and besides this I bought two bed-covers for 4 florins less 10 stivers. I have made the portrait of Nicolas, the jeweller. These are the number of times that I have dined at Bergen since I came from Zeeland ||||||||, and once

for 4 stivers. I paid the driver 3 stivers and spent
8 stivers, and came back to Antwerp, to Jobst
Planckfelt's, on Friday after St. Lucy's, 1520, and
I have dined this number of times with him ||||.
It is paid, and my wife ||||, and that is paid.

AT ANTWERP

December, 1520 – April, 1521

IN return for the three books which I gave him
Herr Lazarus of Ravensburg has given me a
big fish scale, five snail shells, four silver med-
als, five copper ones, two little dried fishes and a
white coral, four reed arrows and another white
coral. I changed 1 florin for expenses, and like-
wise 1 crown. I have dined alone so many times ||||
|||||. The factor of Portugal has given me a brown
velvet bag and a box of good electuary; I gave
his boy 3 stivers for wages. I gave 1 Horn florin
for two little panels, but they gave me back 6
stivers. I bought a little monkey for 4 gulden, and
gave 14 stivers for five fish. I paid Jobst 10 stivers
for three dinners; I gave 2 stivers for two tracts;
and 2 stivers to the messenger. I gave Lazarus of
Ravensburg a portrait head on panel which cost
6 stivers, and besides that I have given him eight
sheets of the large copper engravings, eight of the
half-sheets, an engraved "Passion," and other engravings and woodcuts, all together worth more

than 4 florins. I changed a Philip's florin for expenses, and besides that a gold florin for expenses.
I gave 6 stivers for a panel, and did the portrait of
the servant of the Portuguese on it in charcoal,
and I gave him all that for a New Year's present
and 2 stivers for a tip.

Changed 1 florin for expenses and gave Bernhard Stecher a whole set of prints. I bought 31
stivers' worth of wood. I have made the portraits
of Gerhard Bombelli and Sebastian the procurator's daughter. I have changed 1 florin for expenses. Have spent 3 stivers besides 3 more for
a meal. I have given Herr Wolff of Rogendorf a
"Passion" on copper and one in woodcut. Gerhard Bombelli has given me a printed Turkish
cloth, and Herr Wolff of Rogendorf gave me
seven Brabant ells of velvet, so I gave his man 1
Philip's florin for a tip. Spent 3 stivers on a meal;
gave 4 stivers for tips. I have drawn the new
factor's portrait in charcoal. Gave 6 stivers for a
panel. Have dined with the Portuguese ||||||||
times, with the treasurer |, with Tomasin ||||||||||
times. Gave 4 stivers for tips. With Lazarus of
Ravensburg |, Wolff of Rogendorf |, Bernhard Ste-
cher |, Utz Hanolt Meyting |, Caspar Lewenter |.
I gave 3 stivers to the man whose portrait I drew;
gave the boy 2 stivers. I have given 4 florins for
flax. Have taken 4 florins for prints; have changed
1 crown for expenses. Paid the furrier 4 stivers and
again 2 stivers. Lost 4 stivers at play; spent 6 sti-

vers. I have changed 1 noble for expenses; gave 18 stivers for raisins and three pairs of knives. I paid 2 florins for some meals at Jobst's. Have lost 4 stivers at play, and gave 6 stivers to the furrier. Have given Master Jacob two engraved "St. Jeromes." Lost 2 stivers at play; changed 1 crown for expenses; lost 1 stiver at play. Have given to Tomasin's three maids three pairs of knives, which cost 5 stivers. Have taken 29 stivers for prints. Rodrigo gave me a musk-ball just as it had been cut from the musk deer, also a ¼ lb. of persin [? a dark red paint] and a box full of quince electuary and a big box of sugar, so I gave his boy 5 stivers for a tip.

Lost 2 stivers at play. I have done the portrait of Jobst's wife in charcoal. I have got 4 florins, 5 stivers for three small canvases. Changed 2 florins in succession for expenses. Lost 2 stivers at play. My wife gave me 1 florin for the child, and 4 stivers in the child's bed. I have changed 1 crown for expenses; spent 4 stivers, lost 2 stivers at play, and gave 4 stivers to the messenger. Changed 1 florin for expenses.

I gave Master Dietrich, the glass painter, an "Apocalypse" and the six "Knots." Paid 40 stivers for flax. Lost 8 stivers at play. I have given the little Portuguese factor, Signor Francisco, my small canvas with the small child, that is worth 10 florins. I have given Dr. Loffen at Antwerp the four books and an engraved "Jerome," and the same to Jobst Planckfelt. I have done the arms of Staiber and another. I have made a portrait of Tomasin's son and daughter in silverpoint; also I have painted a small panel in oil of the Duke. Have got 3 stivers for engravings. Rodrigo, the Portuguese secretary, has given me two Calicut cloths, one of them is silk, and he has given me an ornamented cap and a green jug with myrobalans, and a branch of cedar tree, worth 10 florins altogether. And I gave the boy for a tip 5 stivers and 2 stivers for a brush.

I have made a drawing for a mask for the Fugger's people for masquerade, and they have given me an angel. I have changed 1 florin for expenses. Gave 8 stivers for two little powder horns. Lost 3 stivers at play. Changed an angel for expenses. I have drawn two sheets full of beautiful little masks for Tomasin. I have painted a good "Veronica" face in oils; it is worth 12 florins. I gave it to Francisco, the Portuguese factor. Since then I have painted Santa Veronica in oils; it is better than the former, and I gave it to Factor Brandan of Portugal. Francisco gave the maid 1 Philip's florin for a tip, and afterwards, because of the "Veronica," 1 florin more, but the Factor Brandan gave her 1 florin. I paid Peter 8 stivers for two cases. I changed an angel for expenses.

On Carnival Sunday early, the goldsmiths invited me to dinner, with my wife. In their assembly were many notable men. They prepared a very grand meal, and did me the greatest honour. In the evening the old bailiff of the town invited me and gave me a splendid meal, and did me great honour. Thither came many strange maskers.

I have drawn the portrait of Florent Nepotis, Lady Margaret's organist, in charcoal. On Monday night Herr Lopez invited me to the great banquet on Shrove Tuesday, which lasted till two o'clock, and was very grand. Herr Lorenz Sterk has given me a Spanish fur. And to the abovementioned feast came many very splendid masks, especially Tomasin Bombelli.

I have won 2 florins at play. Have changed an angel for expenses; paid 14 stivers for a basket of raisins. I have made the portrait in charcoal of Bernhard von Castell, from whom I won the money. Tomasin's brother Gerhardt has given me four Brabant ells of the best black satin, and has given me three big boxes of candied citron, so I gave the maid 3 stivers for a tip. Paid 13 stivers for wood, and 2 stivers for pine kernels. I drew the procurator's daughter very carefully in silverpoint. Have changed 1 angel for expenses. I have drawn the portrait in black chalk of the good marble worker, Master Johann, who looks like Christopher Kohler; he has studied in Italy, and comes from Metz. I have changed 1 Horn florin for expenses. I have given 3 florins to Jan Türck for Italian works of art; I gave him 12 ducats' worth

works of art for one ounce of good ultramarine. I
have sold a small woodcut of the "Passion" for 3
florins. I sold two reams and four books of Schaüf-
lein's prints for 3 florins. Have given 3 florins for
two ivory salt-cellars from Calicut. Have taken
2 florins for prints; have changed 1 florin for expenses. Rudiger von Gelern gave me a snail shell,
together with coins of gold and silver, with an
ort. I gave him in return the three large books
and an engraved "Knight;" have taken 11 stivers
for prints. I gave 2 Philip's florins for "SS. Peter
and Paul," which I shall present to Herr Kohler's
wife. Rodrigo has given me two boxes of quince
electuary and all kinds of sweetmeats, and I gave
5 stivers for a tip. Paid 16 stivers for boxes.

Lazarus of Ravensburg gave me a sugar loaf,
so I gave his boy 1 stiver. Paid 6 stivers for wood.
Have eaten once with the Frenchman; twice with
the Hirschvogel's Fritz, and once with Master
Peter, the secretary, when Erasmus of Rotterdam
also dined with us. I paid 1 stiver to be allowed to
go up the tower at Antwerp, which is said to be
higher than that at Strasburg. From thence I saw
the whole town on all sides, which was very
pleasant. Paid 1 stiver for a bath. Have changed
1 angel for expenses. The Factor Brandon of Portugal has given me two large beautiful white
sugar loaves, a dishful of sweetmeats, two green
pots of preserves, and four ells of black satin, so
I gave the servant 10 stivers for a tip.

Paid the messenger 3 stivers. I have drawn twice
more in silverpoint the beautiful maiden for Gerhardt. Again changed an angel for expenses; took
4 florins for prints; paid 10 stivers for Rodrigo's
case. Dined with the treasurer, Herr Lorenz Sterk,
who gave me an ivory whistle and a very beautiful piece of porcelain, and I have given him
a whole set of prints. I also gave a whole set
to Herr Adrian, the Antwerp town-orator. Also I
changed a Philip's florin for expenses.

I presented a sitting "St. Nicolas" to the largest
and richest guild of merchants at Antwerp, for
which they have made me a present of 3 Philip's florins. I gave Peter Ægidius the old frame of
the "St. Jerome" besides 4 gulden for a frame for
the treasurer's likeness. Paid 11 stivers for wood.
Again changed a Philip's florin for expenses.
Gave 4 stivers for a bore. Gave 3 stivers for three
canes. I have handed over my bale to Jacob and
Andreas Hessler to take to Nuremberg, and I am
to pay them 2 florins per cwt., Nuremberg weight,
and they are to take it to Herr Hans Imhof, the
elder, and I have paid 2 florins on it. Moreover I
have done it up in a packing-case.

This was in the year 1521, on the Saturday before Judicæ. Also on the Saturday before Judicæ,
Rodrigo gave me six large Indian cocoanuts, a
very fine piece of coral, and two large Portuguese
florins, one of which weighs 10 ducats, and I gave
the boy 15 stivers for a tip.

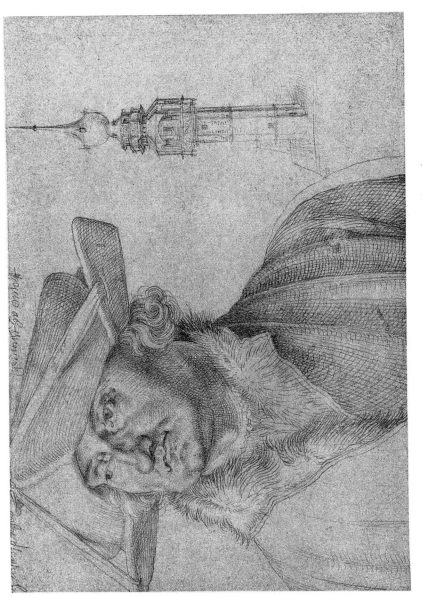

Lazarus Ravensburger; a Tower in Antwerp. Silverpoint.

*Katherina. 1521. (The African servant of the commercial represen-
tative of the King of Portugal ["Factor Brandon" in the text].)*

I have bought a lode-stone for 16 stivers. I have changed an angel for expenses. Paid 6 stivers for packing. Sent Master Hugo at Brussels an engraved "Passion" and some other prints for his little porphyry stone. I have made for Tomasin a design drawn and tinted in half-colours, from which he means to have his house painted. I painted "Jerome" in oils with care and gave it to Rodrigo of Portugal, who gave Susanna a ducat for a tip. Have changed a Philip's florin for expenses and gave 10 stivers to my Father Confessor. Gave 4 stivers for the little tortoise.

I have dined with Herr Gilbert, who gave me a Calicut target made of a fish skin, and two gloves as they use them for fighting. I have given Peter 2 stivers. Gave 10 stivers for the fish fins, and 3 stivers for a tip. I have made a very good portrait in hard chalk of Cornelius, the secretary of Antwerp. I have given 3 florins, 16 stivers, for the five silk girdles which I mean to give away, besides 20 stivers for an edging [? lace]. These six edgings I have sent as presents to the wives of Kasperi Nützel, Franz Imhof, Straüb, the two Spenglers, Löffelhölz, besides a good pair of gloves to each. To Pirkheimer I have sent a large cap, a very handsome buffalo horn inkstand, a silver [medal of the] Emperor, a pound of pistachios, and three sugar-canes. To Kasper Nützel I have sent a great elk's foot, ten large fir cones with pine kernels. To Jacob Muffel I have sent a scarlet breast cloth of one ell; to Hans Imhof's child an embroidered scarlet cap and pine kernels; to Kramer's wife four ells of taffeta, worth 4 florins. To Lochinger's wife one ell of taffeta, of 1 florin's worth; to the two Spenglers, each a bag and three fine horns; to Herr Hieronimus Holzschuher, a very large horn. Have eaten twice with the factor; dined with Master Adrian, the secretary of the town council of Antwerp, who gave me the small painted panel made by Master Joachim [de Patinir]: it is of "Lot and his Daughters." Have taken 12 florins for prints, also I have sold some of Hans Baldung Grün's works for 1 florin. Rudiger von Gelern has given me a piece of sandalwood; I gave his boy a stiver. I have painted the portrait of Bernhard of Brussels in oils; he gave me 8 florins for it, and gave my wife a crown, and Susanna a florin worth 24 stivers. I have given 3 stivers for the Swiss jug, and 2 stivers for the ship, also 3 stivers for the case and 4 stivers to the Father Confessor. I have changed an angel for expenses; have taken 4 florins, 10 stivers for works of art; paid 3 stivers for salve; gave 12½ stivers for wood; changed 1 florin for expenses; have given 1 florin for 14 pieces of French wood. I gave Ambrozio Hochstütter a "Life of Our Lady," and he gave me a model of his ship. Rodrigo gave my wife a little ring which is worth more than 5 florins. Have changed 1 florin for expenses. I have done the portrait of Factor Brandon's secretary in char-

76

coal; I have done the portrait of his Moorish woman in silverpoint, and I have done Rodrigo's portrait on a large sheet of paper with the brush, in black and white. I have given 16 florins for a piece of camlet measuring twenty-four ells, and it cost 1 stiver to bring home. Have paid 2 stivers for gloves. I have done Lucas of Dantzic's portrait in charcoal. He gave me 1 florin for it, and a piece of sandalwood.

VISIT TO BRUGES AND GHENT

April 6–11, 1521

ON the Saturday after Easter, with Hans Lüber and Master Jan Prevost, a good painter born at Bruges, I set out from Antwerp towards Bruges by way of the Scheldt and came to Beveren, a large village. From there to Vracene, also a big village; thence we passed through some villages and came to a fine large village, where the rich farmers live, and there we breakfasted. Thence we journeyed towards St. Paul's, the rich abbey, and went through Caudenborn, a fine village; thence through the large village of Kalve, and thence to Ertvelde; there we lay the night and started early on Sunday morning and came from Ertvelde to a small town. From that we went to Ecloo, which is a mighty large village; it is plastered, and has a square;

there we breakfasted. Thence we went to Maldegem, and then through other villages, and came to Bruges, which is a fine noble town. I paid 21 stivers for fare and other expenses. And arriving at Bruges, Jan Prevost took me into his house to lodge, and the same night prepared a costly meal, and asked much company to meet me. The next day Marx, the goldsmith, invited me, and gave me a costly meal and asked many to meet me; afterwards they took me to see the Emperor's house, which is large and splendid. There I saw the chapel which Roger painted, and some pictures by a great old artist. I gave the man who showed them to us 1 stiver; afterwards I bought two ivory combs for 30 stivers. Thence they took me to St. James's and let me see the splendid paintings of Roger and Hugo, who are both great masters. Afterwards I saw the alabaster Madonna in Our Lady's Church that Michelangelo of Rome made; afterwards they took me to many churches and let me see all the fine paintings, of which there is abundance there, and when I had seen the Jan [Van Eyck] and all the other things, we came at last to the Painters' Chapel, in which there are good things. Then they prepared a banquet for me, and I went thence with them to their guildhall; there were many honourable men gathered together, goldsmiths, painters, and merchants, and they made me sup with them, and they gave me presents and sought my acquaintance and did me great honour; and the two brothers Jacob and Peter Mostaert, the town councillors, gave me twelve cans of wine, and the whole assembly, more than sixty persons, accompanied me home with many torches. I also saw in their shooting gallery the great fish tub from which they eat, which is 19 feet long, 7 high, and 7 broad.

Early on Tuesday we departed, but before that, I did Jan Prevost's portrait in silverpoint, and gave his wife 10 stivers at parting. And so we travelled to Ursel; there we breakfasted. On the way there are three villages. Then we travelled towards Ghent, again through three villages, and I paid 4 stivers for the journey, and 4 stivers for expenses; and on my arrival at Ghent, there came to me the dean of the painters and brought with him the first masters in painting; they showed me great honour, received me most courteously, and commended to me their good-will and service, and supped with me. On Wednesday early they took me to the tower of St. John's, whence I looked all over the great and wonderful town, where I had just been treated as a great person. Afterwards I saw the Jan [Van Eyck's] picture, which is a very splendid, deeply studied painting, and especially the "Eve," the "Mary," and "God the Father" were extremely good. Then I saw the lions and drew one of them in silverpoint; also I saw on the bridge, where men are beheaded, two

pictures which were made as a sign that there a
son had beheaded his father. Ghent is beautiful
and a wonderful town; four great waters flow
through it. I gave 3 stivers as a tip to the sacris-
tan and the lions' keeper. I saw many other remarkable things in Ghent, and the painters with
their dean did not forget me, but ate with me
morning and evening, and paid for everything,
and were very friendly. I gave away 5 stivers at
the inn on leaving. Then early on Thursday I set
out from Ghent and came through various villages to the inn called "The Swan," where we
breakfasted; thence we passed through a beautiful village and came to Antwerp, and I paid 8
stivers for the fare.

AT ANTWERP

April 11 – May 17, 1521

I HAVE taken 4 florins for works of art; changed
one florin for expenses. Have taken the portrait of Hans Lieber of Ulm in charcoal; he
wished to pay me 1 florin, but I would not take
it. Gave 7 stivers for wood and 1 stiver for bringing it; changed 1 florin for expenses. In the third
week after Easter a violent fever came upon me
with great weakness, nausea, and headache; and
before, when I was in Zeeland, a strange illness
overcame me such as I never heard of from

anyone, and this illness I have still. I paid 6 stivers
for a case. The monk has bound two books for
me for the prints which I gave him. I have given
10 florins, 8 stivers for a piece of arras for two
mantles for my mother-in-law and my wife. I
gave the doctor 8 stivers, and 3 stivers to the
apothecary, also changed 1 florin for expenses
and spent 3 stivers in company. Paid the doctor 10 stivers; again paid the doctor 6 stivers.
During my illness Rodrigo sent me many sweetmeats; I gave the boy 4 stivers for a tip. I have
drawn Master Joachim [Patinir] in silverpoint,
and made him besides another likeness in silverpoint. Again changed a crown for expenses,
and again 1 florin for expenses. Paid the doctor 6 stivers, and 7 stivers at the apothecary's;
changed 1 florin for expenses. For packing the
third bale, which I sent from Antwerp to Nuremberg by a carrier called Hans Staber, I paid
13 stivers, and I paid the carrier 1 florin for it, and
I agreed with him to take it from Antwerp to
Nuremberg for 1 florin, 1 ort, per cwt., and this
bale is to be taken to Herr Hans Imhof, the elder.
I have paid the doctor, the apothecary, and the
barber 14 stivers. I gave Master Jacob, the surgeon, 4 florins' worth of prints. I have made a
portrait in charcoal of Thomas Polonius of Rome.
My camlet cloak came to twenty-one Brabant
ells, which are three finger breadths longer than
the Nuremberg ells. I have also bought four black

Spanish skins, which cost 3 stivers each, and they come to 34, that makes 10 florins, 2 stivers; I paid the skinner [furrier] 1 florin to make them up, then there were two ells of velvet for trimming, 5 florins; also for silk cord and thread, 34 stivers; then the tailor's wage, 30 stivers; the camlet which is in the cloak cost 14½ florins, and the boy 5 stivers for a tip.

Cross Sunday after Easter; from this I start a fresh account. Again paid the doctor 6 stivers; I have gained 53 stivers for works of art, and have taken them for expenses. On Sunday before Holy Cross Week, Master Joachim [Patinir], the good landscape painter, asked me to his wedding, and showed me all honour; there I saw two beautiful plays, the first was especially pious and devout. I again paid the doctor 6 stivers, and have changed 1 florin for expenses. On Sunday after Our Lord's Ascension, Master Dietrich, the glass painter of Antwerp, invited me and asked many other people to meet me, and especially among them Alexander, the goldsmith, a rich, stately man, and we had a splendid dinner, and they did me great honour. I have done in charcoal the portrait of Master Marx, the goldsmith, who lives at Bruges. I bought a broad cap for 36 stivers. I paid Paul Geiger 1 florin to take my little chest to Nuremberg, and 4 stivers for the letter. I have taken the portrait of Ambrosius Hochstätter in charcoal, and I dined with him; I have dined at least six times with Tomasin. I bought some wooden dishes and platters for 3 stivers. I have given the apothecary 12 stivers. I have given two books of the "Life of Our Lady," one to the foreign surgeon, the other to Marx's house servant; I also paid the doctor 8 stivers, and gave 4 stivers for cleaning an old cap. Lost 4 stivers at play; have given 2 florins for a new cap. I have changed the old cap because it was clumsy, and have given 6 stivers more for another. Painted a portrait of the duke in oils; have made a very fine and careful portrait in oils of the treasurer, Lorenz Sterk; it was worth 25 florins. I presented it to him, and in return he gave me 20 florins, and to Susanna 1 florin for a tip. Likewise I painted the portrait of Jobst, my host, very well and carefully in oils; he has now given me [the portrait I did of him before?] and I have done his wife again and painted her portrait in oils.

On the Friday before Whitsuntide, 1521, tidings came to me at Antwerp that Martin Luther had been so treacherously taken prisoner, for he trusted the Emperor Charles's herald, who had been granted to him with the Imperial safe conduct, but as soon as the herald had brought him near Eisenach, to an unfriendly place, he said that he would not need him any more and rode away. Immediately there appeared ten knights, who treacherously carried off the pious man, who had been betrayed; a man enlightened by the Holy

Ghost, a follower of Christ and of the true Christian faith, and whether he lives yet or whether
they have put him to death, I know not. If he
has suffered, it is for the sake of Christian truth
and because he has fought with the un-Christlike
papacy, which strives with its heavy load of human laws against the redemption of Christ; and if
so, it is that we may be again robbed and stripped
of the fruit of our blood and sweat, that the same
may be shamelessly and scandalously squan-
dered by lazy folk while poor and sick men must
therefore die of hunger. And this is above all
most grievous to me, that God perhaps will let
us remain yet under their false, blind doctrine,
invented and set forth by the men whom they
call "Fathers," through whom the Word of God
is in many places falsely expounded or not taught
at all. O God of Heaven, have pity on us, O Lord
Jesus Christ, pray for Thy people. Deliver us in
due time, uphold in us the right and true Christian Faith. Gather together Thy far scattered
sheep by Thy voice, in the Scripture called Thy
godly Word. Help us that we may know this Thy
voice and may follow no other deceiving call of
human error, that we may not, Lord Jesus Christ,
fall away from Thee. Call together again the
sheep of Thy pasture, who are still in part found
in the Roman Church, and with them, too, the
Indians, Muscovites, Russians, and Greeks, who
have been thus cut off by the oppression and

pride of the pope and by false appearance of ho-
liness. O God, redeem thy poor folk constrained
by heavy ban and edict which it no wise willingly obeys, whereby it is bound continually to
sin against its conscience if it disobeys them. O
God, never hast Thou so heavily burdened a people under human laws as us poor ones beneath
the Roman chair, who daily long to be free Chris-
tians ransomed by Thy blood. O Highest Heavenly Father, pour into our hearts through Thy
Son Jesus Christ such a light, that we may know
thereby which messenger we are to obey, so
that with good conscience we may lay aside the
burdens of others, and may serve Thee, Eternal
Heavenly Father, with free and joyful heart. And
if we lose this man, who has written more clearly
than anyone in a hundred and forty years, and to
whom Thou hast given such an evangelic spirit,
we pray Thee, O Heavenly Father, that Thou
give again Thy spirit to another, that he may
gather together anew from all parts the holy
Christian Church, that we may all live again in
a pure and Christian manner, so that from our
good works all unbelievers, with Turks, heathens,
and Calicuts, may turn themselves to us and
embrace the Christian faith. But, Lord, Thou
willest, ere Thou judgest, that as Thy Son Jesus
Christ was constrained to die by the hands of the
priests and rise from the dead and after to ascend
to heaven, that so too, in like manner, it should

be with Thy follower, Martin Luther, whose life
the pope compasses, with money, treacherously
towards God, him, Thou wilt quicken again. And
as Thou, Lord, ordainedst that Jerusalem should
be destroyed, so wilt Thou also destroy this self-
assumed authority of the Roman chair. O Lord,
give us thereafter the new beautified Jerusalem, which descends from heaven, whereof the
Apocalypse writes, the holy pure gospel which
is not darkened by human doctrine.

Whoever reads Martin Luther's books may see
how clear and transparent his doctrine is, for he
teaches the Holy Gospel. Wherefore his writings
are to be held in the greatest honour, and not to
be burned; unless, indeed, his opponents, who always fight against the truth, were also cast into
the fire with all their opinions, they who would
make gods out of men, but then only if there
were printed new Lutheran books. "O God, if
Luther be dead, who will henceforth expound
the Holy Gospel so clearly to us! Ah, God, what
might he not have written for us in the next ten or
twenty years!" "Oh, all ye pious Christian men,
help me to lament this God-inspired man and
pray to Him that He will send us another enlightened man. Oh, Erasmus of Rotterdam, where wilt
thou stay? Dost thou see how the unjust tyranny
of worldly power and the might of darkness prevail? Hear, thou knight of Christ, ride on beside
the Lord Jesus; guard the truth, win the martyr's

crown! Thou art already only a little old man, and I have heard thee say that thou givest thy-self but two years more in which thou mayest avail to accomplish something. Lay out the same now well for the gospel and the true Christian Faith and make thyself heard, so shall the gates of hell, the Roman Chair, as Christ says, in no wise prevail against thee; and if here, like thy Master Christ, thou wert to suffer shame at the hands of the liars of this time and therefore wert to die a little sooner, the sooner wouldst thou come from death into life and be glorified through Christ. For if thou drinkest out of the cup whereof He drank, with Him thou shalt reign, and judge with justice those who have dealt unrighteously. Oh, Erasmus, hold to this, that God may be thy praise, even as it is written of David, for verily thou mayest overthrow Goliath. For God stands by the Holy Christian Church, as He only up-holds the Romish Church according to His Godly will [text here corrupt]. May He help us to ever-lasting happiness, Who is God the Father, the Son, and the Holy Ghost, one God, Amen. Oh, ye Christian men, pray God for help, for His judge-ment draws near and His justice shall appear. Then shall we behold the innocent blood which the pope, priests, bishops, and monks have shed, judged and condemned. Apocalypse: "These are the slain who lie beneath the altar of God and cry for vengeance, to whom the voice of

God answers, Await the full number of the inno-cent slain, then will I judge."

Again changed 1 florin for expenses, and gave the doctor 8 stivers; dined twice with Rodrigo; dined with the rich canon; changed 1 florin for ex-penses. I had Master Conrad, the sculptor of Mech-lin, as a guest on Whitsunday; paid 18 stivers for Italian prints: again 6 stivers to the doctor. For Master Joachim I have drawn four "St. Christo-phers" on grey paper, heightened with white. On the last day of Whitsuntide I was at Antwerp at the great yearly horse-fair; there I saw a great number of beautiful stallions ridden, and two stallions in particular were sold for 700 florins. I have taken 1 florin, 3 ort, for prints and used the money for expenses; 4 stivers to the doctor, 3 stivers for two little books. I have dined thrice with Tomasin. I have designed three dagger grips for him, and he gave me a small alabaster bowl. I have taken the portrait in charcoal of an English nobleman, who gave me 1 florin which I changed for expenses. Master Gerhardt, the min-iature painter, has a daughter about eighteen years old, called Susanna, who has illuminated a little page with a Saviour, for which I gave her 1 florin. It is very wonderful that a woman's picture should be so good. Have lost 6 stivers at play. I saw the great procession at Antwerp on Holy Trinity Day. Master Conrad has given me a beautiful pair of knives, and so I gave his

88

little old man a "Life of Our Lady" in return. I have taken the portrait in charcoal of Johann, the Brussels goldsmith, likewise his wife's. I have received 2 florins for prints, also Master Johann, the Brussels goldsmith, paid me 3 Philip's florins for what I did for him, namely, the drawing for the seal and the two portraits. I have given the "Veronica" which I painted in oils, and the "Adam and Eve" that Franz did to Johann, the goldsmith, in return for a jacinth and an agate with a Lucrecia engraved in it. Each of us valued his portion at 14 florins. Further, I gave him a whole set of engravings for a ring and six stones; each valued his portion at 7 florins. Gave 14 stivers for two pairs of gloves; gave 2 stivers for two small boxes; changed 2 Philip's florins for expenses. I drew three "Bearing of the Cross" and two "Mount of Olives" on five half-sheets. I have taken three portraits in black and white on grey paper, also I drew in black and white on grey paper, two Netherlandish costumes. For the Englishman I have painted his arms in colours, for which he gave me 1 florin. Besides this, one way and another, I have done many drawings and other things to serve people, and for the greater part of my work I have received nothing. Andreas of Cracow paid me 1 Philip's florin for a shield and a child's head. Changed 1 florin for expenses. Have given 2 stivers for sweeping brushes. At Antwerp I saw the great procession on Corpus Christi Day, which was very splendid. Gave 4 stivers for a tip and 6 stivers to the doctor; changed 1 florin for expenses; 1 stiver for a box. Have dined five times with Tomasin; paid 10 stivers to the apothecary and to his wife 14 stivers for the clyster, and 15 stivers to him for the prescription. Again changed 2 Philip's florins for expenses; 6 stivers again to the doctor, and once more 10 stivers for a clyster to the apothecary's wife, and 4 stivers to the apothecary. I gave the monk who confessed my wife 8 stivers. I have given 8 florins for a whole piece of arras, and again for fourteen ells of fine arras, 8 florins; the apothecary 32 stivers for medicines; to the messenger I have given 3 stivers and the tailor 4 stivers. I have dined once with Hans Fehler, and thrice with Tomasin. Gave 10 stivers for packing. On the Wednesday after Corpus Christi in the year 1521, I gave over my great bale at Antwerp to be sent to Nuremberg, to the carrier, by name Kunz Metz of Schlaudersdorf, and I am to pay him for carrying it to Nuremberg 1½ florins for every cwt., and I paid him 1 gulden on account, and he is to hand it over to Herr Hans Imhof, the elder. I have done the portrait of young Jacob Rehlinger at Antwerp; have dined three times with Tomasin.

On the eighth day after Corpus Christi I went with my wife to Mechlin to Lady Margaret; took 5 florins with me for expenses; my wife changed

1 florin for expenses. At Mechlin I lodged with Master Heinrich, the painter, at the sign of the Golden Head. The painters and sculptors made me their guest at my inn, and did me great honour in their gathering; and I visited the Poppenreuter's, the gun-maker's house, and found wonderful things there. And I have been to Lady Margaret's, and I let her see my Kaiser, and would have presented it to her, but she disliked it so much that I took it away again. And on Friday Lady Margaret showed me all her beautiful things, and among them I saw about forty small pictures in oils, the like of which for cleanness and excellence I have never seen. And there I saw other good works by Jan [Van Eyck] and Jacopo [de' Barbari]. I asked my lady for Jacopo's little book, but she said she had promised it to her painter; then I saw many other costly things and a fine library. Master Hans Poppenreuter invited me as his guest. I have had Master Conrad twice, and his wife once, as my guests, also the chamberlain Stephen and his wife, both as guests. 27 stivers and 2 stivers for fare. I have taken in charcoal the portrait of Stephen, the chamberlain, and Master Conrad, the carver, and on Saturday I came back from Mechlin to Antwerp.

My trunk started on the Saturday after Corpus Christi week. Changed 1 florin for expenses, gave the messenger 3 stivers. Dined twice with the Augustines; dined with Alexander Imhof; paid 6 stivers at the apothecary's; dined again with the Augustines. I have drawn in charcoal Master Jacob, and had a little panel made for it, which cost 6 stivers, and gave it to him. I have done the portrait of Bernhard Stecher and his wife, and gave him a whole set of prints, and I took his wife's portrait again, and gave 6 stivers for making the little panel, all of which I gave him, and he in return gave me 10 florins. Master Lucas, who engraves in copper, invited me as his guest. He is a little man, born at Leyden, in Holland, and was at Antwerp. I have eaten with Master Bernhard Stecher. Gave 1½ stivers to the messenger; have taken 1 florin, 1 ort, for prints. I have drawn Master Lucas von Leyden in silverpoint. I have lost 1 florin; paid the doctor 6 stivers and again 6 stivers. I gave the steward of the Augustines' Convent at Antwerp a "Life of Our Lady," and 4 stivers to his man. I have given Master Jacob a copper "Passion" and a wood "Passion," and five other pieces, and 4 stivers to his man; have changed 4 florins for expenses; gave 2 Philip's florins for fourteen fish skins; made portraits in black chalk of Art Braun and his wife. I gave the goldsmith who valued the ring for me 1 florin's worth of prints; of the three rings which I took in exchange for prints, the two smaller are valued at 15 crowns, but the sapphire at 25 crowns; that makes 54 florins, 8 stivers; and what, amongst other things, the above Frenchman took

The Artist Lucas van Leyden. 1521. Silverpoint.

King Christian II of Denmark. 1521. Charcoal on yellowed paper.

was thirty-six large books, which makes 9 florins. Have given 2 stivers for a screw knife.

The man with the three rings has overreached
me by a half. I understood nothing in the matter.
I gave 18 stivers for a red cap for my godchild;
lost 12 stivers at play; drank 2 stivers, bought
three fine small rubies for 11 gold florins, 12 stivers;
changed 1 florin for expenses. Dined again with
the Augustines; dined twice with Tomasin. I gave
6 stivers for thirteen porpoise-bristle brushes, and
3 stivers for six bristle brushes. I have made a
careful portrait in black chalk on a royal sheet
of the great Anthony Hainault, and I have done
careful portraits in black chalk of Braun and his
wife on royal sheets, and I have done another one
of him in silverpoint; he has given me an angel.
Changed 1 florin for expenses, paid 1 florin for a
pair of shoes; gave 6 stivers for an inkstand. I gave
12 stivers for a case for packing; 21 stivers for one
dozen ladies' gloves; 6 stivers for a bag; 3 stivers
for three bristle brushes; changed 1 florin for expenses; gave 1 stiver for a piece of fine red leather.
Anthony Hainault, whose portrait I did, has given
me 3 Philip's florins, and Bernhard Stecher has
made me a present of a tortoise shell; I have
done the portrait of his wife's niece; dined once
with her husband and he gave me 2 Philip's
florins; gave 1 stiver for a tip. I have given Anthony Hainault two books; received 13 stivers for
prints. I have given Master Joachim the Hans

Grün woodcut. I have changed 3 Philip's florins for expenses; dined twice with Bernhard Stecher; again twice with Tomasin. I have given Jobst's wife four woodcuts; gave Friedrich, Jobst's man, two large books; gave glazier Hennick's son two books. Rodrigo gave me one of the parrots which they bring from Malacca, and I gave his man 5 stivers for a tip. Again dined twice with Tomasin; have given 2 stivers for a little cage, 3 stivers for one pair of socks, and 4 stivers for eight little boards. I gave Peter two whole sheet engravings and one sheet of woodcut. Again dined twice with Tomasin; changed 1 florin for expenses. I gave Master Art, the glass painter, a "Life of Our Lady," and I gave Master Jean, the French sculptor, a whole set of prints; he gave my wife six little glasses with rose water; they are very finely made. Bought a packing-case for 7 stivers; changed 1 florin for expenses; have given 7 stivers for a cut [leather] bag. Cornelius, the secretary, has given me Luther's "Babylonian Captivity;" in return I gave him my three big books. I gave Peter Puz, the monk, one florin's worth of prints; to the glass painter, Hennick, I gave two large books; gave 4 stivers for a piece of glazed calico; changed 1 Philip's florin for expenses. I gave 8 florins' worth of my prints for a whole set of Lucas's engravings; again changed 1 Philip's florin for expenses. I gave 8 stivers for a bag and 7 stivers for half a dozen Netherlandish cards, and 3 stivers for a

small yellow post-horn. I paid 24 stivers for meat,
12 stivers for coarse cloth, and again 5 stivers for
coarse cloth. Have eaten twice with Tomasin. I
gave 1 stiver to Peter; gave 7 stivers for a present and 3 stivers for sacking. Rodrigo has presented me with six ells of coarse black cloth for a
cape; it cost a crown an ell. Changed 2 florins for
expenses; gave the tailor's man 2 stivers for a tip.
I have reckoned up with Jobst and I owe him 31
florins, which I paid him. Therein were charged
and deducted two portrait heads which I painted
in oils, for which he gave me five pounds of borax,
Netherlandish weight.

In all my doings, spendings, sales, and other
dealings in the Netherlands, in all my affairs with
high and low, I have suffered loss, and Lady
Margaret in particular gave me nothing for what
I gave her and did for her. This settlement with
Jobst was made on SS. Peter and Paul's Day. I
gave Rodrigo's man 7 stivers for a tip. I have
given Master Hennick an engraved "Passion;" he
gave me some burning pastilles. I had to pay the
tailor 25 stivers for making up the cape. I have
engaged a carrier to take me from Antwerp to
Cologne. I am to pay him 13 light florins, each
of 24 stivers, and am to pay besides the expenses
for a man and a boy. Jacob Rehlinger has given
me 1 ducat for his charcoal portrait. Gerhard has
given me two little pots with capers and olives,
for which I gave 4 stivers as a tip. Gave Rodrigo's

man 1 stiver. I have given my portrait of the Emperor in exchange for a white English cloth which Jacob, Tomasin's son-in-law, gave me. Alexander Imhof has lent me a full hundred gold florins, on the Eve of Our Lady's Crossing the Mountains, 1521. For this I have given him my sealed signature, which he will have presented to me at Nuremberg, when I will pay him back with thanks. Gave 6 stivers for a pair of shoes; paid the apothecary 11 stivers, paid 3 stivers for cord. In Tomasin's kitchen I gave away a Philip's florin in leaving gifts, and I gave his maiden daughter a gold florin on leaving. I have dined thrice with him. I gave Jobst's wife a florin and 1 florin in the kitchen for leaving gifts, also I gave 2 stivers to the packers. Tomasin has given me a small jar full of the best theriac. Changed 3 florins for expenses; gave the house servant 10 stivers on leaving; gave Peter 1 stiver; gave 2 stivers for a tip. I gave 3 stivers to Master Jacob's man; 4 stivers for sacking; gave Peter 1 stiver; gave the messenger 3 stivers.

On Our Lady's Visitation, when I was just leaving Antwerp, the King of Denmark sent for me to come to him at once, to do his portrait; this I did in charcoal, and I did the portrait, too, of his servant Anthony, and I had to dine with the King, who showed himself very gracious to me. I have entrusted my bale to Leonhard Tucher and given over to him my white cloth. The car-

rier with whom I bargained, did not take me; I
fell out with him. Gerhard has given me some
Italian seeds. I gave the new carrier to take home
the great turtle shell, the fish shield, the long
pipe, the long shield, the fish fins, and the two
little casks of lemons and capers, on Our Lady's
Visitation Day, 1521.

Next day we set out for Brussels on the King
of Denmark's business, and I engaged a driver,
to whom I gave 2 florins. I presented to the King
of Denmark the best pieces of all my prints,
they are worth 5 florins. Changed 2 florins for expenses; paid 1 stiver for a dish and basket. I saw,
too, how the people of Antwerp wondered very
much when they saw the King of Denmark, that
he was such a manly, handsome man, and that
he had come hither with only two companions
through his enemies' country. I saw, too, how the
Emperor rode forth from Brussels to meet him
and received him honourably and with great
pomp. Then I saw the noble costly banquet that
the Emperor and Lady Margaret held next day.
Paid 2 stivers for a pair of gloves. Herr Anthony
paid me 12 Horn florins, of which I gave 2 Horn
florins to the painter for the little panel to paint
the portrait on, and 2 Horn florins for having colours rubbed for me; the other 8 Horn florins I took
for expenses. On the Sunday before St. Margaret's Day, the King of Denmark gave a great banquet to the Emperor, Lady Margaret, and the

Queen of Spain, and invited me, and I dined there also. Paid 12 stivers for the King's frame, and I painted the King in oils,—he has given me 30 florins. I gave 2 stivers to the young man called Bartholomew, who rubbed the colours for me; I bought a little glass jar which once belonged to the King for 2 stivers. Paid 2 stivers for a tip; gave 2 stivers for the engraved goblets. I have given Master Jan's boy four half-sheets, and to the master-painter's boy an "Apocalypse" and four half-sheets. Thomas of Bologna has given me one or two Italian prints; I have also bought one for 1 stiver. Master Jobst, the tailor, invited me and I supped with him. I have paid for the hire of a room at Brussels for eight days, 32 stivers. I have given an engraved "Passion" to the wife of Master Jan, the goldsmith, with whom I dined three times. I gave another "Life of Our Lady" to Bartholomew, the painter's apprentice; I have dined with Herr Nicolas Ziegler, and gave 1 stiver to Master Jan's servant. Because of being unable to get a carriage, I have stayed on two days in Brussels; paid 1 stiver for a pair of socks.

On Friday morning early I started from Brussels, and I am to pay the driver 10 florins. I paid my hostess 5 stivers more for the single night. From there we rode through two villages and came to Louvain; breakfasted, and spent 13 stivers. Thence we journeyed through three villages and came to Thienen, which is a little town, and lay the night there, and I spent 9 stivers. From there, early on St. Margaret's Day, we travelled through two villages and came to a town which is called St. Truyen, where they are building a large, well-designed church tower, quite new. From thence we went on past some poor houses and came to a little town, Tongeren; there we had our morning meal, and spent all together, 6 stivers. From thence we went through a village and some poor houses and came to Maestricht, where I lay the night, and spent 12 stivers, and 2 blanke besides, for watch money. Thence we journeyed early on Sunday to Aachen, where we ate and spent all together 14 stivers. Thence we travelled to Altenburg, taking six hours, because the driver did not know the way and went wrong; there we stayed for the night and spent 6 stivers. On Monday early we travelled through Jülich, a town, and came to Bergheim, where we ate and drank, and spent 3 stivers. Thence we journeyed through three more villages and came to Cologne.

Translated by Rudolph Tombo, Ph.D.

NOTES

To the Introduction

Page ix, line 11. "power."
"I saw also that Death smote her two great strokes to the heart."

Page xiv, line 29. "representation."
Nothing in Dürer's engraved work can compare for unity and expressive purposefulness of disposition with Schongauer's engraving of the Virgin and Child.

Page xvii, line 16. "design."
It is only fair to state that in the Genius of Time the empty and inflated drapery over the chest in the original is greatly improved by Dürer, who gives the torso more plastic relief, but even here the relation of the body to the legs lacks the continuity of the Tarrocchi engraving.

Page xxiii, line 11. "art."
Some caution, however, is necessary here, for one of the drawings that upon internal evidences of style we should most certainly have attributed to the period of Dürer's stay in the Netherlands is now known to represent Paul Hofhaimer, the court organist, whom he met at Augsburg in 1518. It would almost seem as though the attraction of Netherlandish art had already begun to work upon him before the journey took place.

Page 3, line 13. "Those."

Opinions differ as to whether this refers to the Germans, or to the Italian shopkeepers on the Riva.

Page 4, line 5. "debt."

Pirkheimer had lent Dürer money for the Italian journey.

Page 4, line 8. "Germans."

This is the "Madonna of the Rose Garlands," painted for the chapel of S. Bartolommeo, the burial-place of the German colony. About the year 1600 it was bought for a high price by the Emperor Rudolf II, who is said to have had it carried by four men all the way to Prague to avoid the risk of damage in transport. It now belongs to the Strahow monastery at Prague. It has suffered serious damage, but still remains one of the most important of all Dürer's works.

Page 4, line 10. "five."

How far out he was in his calculations will be seen from subsequent letters.

Page 4, line 20. "art."

That is, the engravings and woodcuts from which Dürer drew a steady income throughout his artistic career.

Page 4, line 22. "Pfinzing."

Pfinzing had lent Dürer 118 gulden on the security of his father's house.

Page 5, line 16. "wont."
Dürer's portrait of his prematurely aged mother fully confirms this observation.

Page 6, line 22. "Bellini."
The character of Bellini agrees with all we know of him. Camerarius tells an amusing story of the two artists, to the effect that Bellini once asked Dürer for one of the brushes with which he painted hairs. Dürer produced several quite ordinary brushes and offered them to Bellini. Bellini replied that he did not mean those, but some brush with the hairs divided which would enable him to draw a number of fine parallel lines such as Dürer did. Dürer assured him that he used no special kind, and proceeded to draw a number of long wavy lines like tresses with such absolute regularity and parallelism that Bellini declared that nothing but seeing it done would have convinced him that such a feat of skill was possible.

Page 6, last line. "thing."
It is impossible to do more than guess at the meaning of this passage. The main difference in Venetian art between 1494, when Dürer was first in Venice, and 1506 was the emergence of Giorgione and the new styles which he, Titian, and Palma were creating. But if Dürer refers here to this, he would hardly have said that Bellini was the best painter of all, since Bellini stood, on the

whole, for the older tradition. Nor indeed would Dürer be likely to be fascinated by a style so far removed from his own. It is more likely that it refers to the same subject as the following sentence, and that the "thing" is some work by Jacopo de' Barbari seen by Dürer eleven years before, and at that time extravagantly admired.

Page 7, line 20. "ninth."
Reckoning from sunset, at this season would be about 2.30 a.m.

To Letter III

Page 8, line 7. "pictures."
Probably small pictures which he brought with him from Nuremberg.

To Letter IV

Page 10, line 7. "marcelli."
A Venetian coin worth 10 soldi.

Page 11, line 11. "again."
That is, on approval.

Page 11, line 21. "Council."
The Town Council of Nuremberg, which apparently watched the careers of Nuremberg students studying abroad.

Page 12, line 9. "ring."
This was the ring mentioned in Letter III. It had
not been ordered by Pirkheimer, but was sent
by Dürer on the chance of its pleasing.

Page 12, line 16. "rings."
The diamond and ruby rings of Letter III, where
they are provisionally valued at 10 ducats.

Page 13, line 11. "School."
The "Scuola" or guild of the painters.
It is a little curious that Dürer should have regarded this as an unfriendly act, since it was an
almost universal rule at this period that foreign
painters must be enrolled in the local school before practising in a town. The Nuremberg guild
may have been less strict.

Page 13, line 15. "Whitsuntide."
It was not finished till September. The price
paid was low considering the size and complexity of the work. Bellini at this time received 100
ducats for a large picture.

Page 13, line 19. "away."
To Nuremberg. Literally "up there."

Page 13, line 26. "Wolgemut."
Michael Wolgemut, Dürer's master.

Page 13, line 27. "brother."
Hans Dürer, who was fifteen at this date. He be-

Notes came a painter of second-rate ability, and afterwards helped Albrecht in the decoration of the Emperor Maximilian's prayer book.

Page 14, line 13. "sell."
That is, Dürer's engravings.

To Letter VI

Page 15, line 4. "ring."
See Letter IV.

Page 15, line 12. "here."
Here follows drawing in the original.

Page 15, line 22. "Imhof."
Hans Imhof, the elder, at Nuremberg; the younger Imhof was in Venice.

To Letter VII

Page 16, line 11. "To."
The first four sentences of this letter were written by Dürer in Italian.

Page 16, line 17. "bullies."
"Tiraisbuli," meaning doubtful.

Page 16, line 22. "Schott's."
Kunz Schott, an enemy of the town of Nuremberg.

Page 17, line 13. "Weisweber."
A Nuremberg general.

Page 18, line 20. "letter."
This letter is not known.

Page 19, line 12. "King."
Maximilian intended to go to Rome, where he was to be crowned Emperor.

To Letter VIII

Page 20, line 5. "Margrave."
Friedrich of Brandenburg.

Page 20, line 22. "Kamerer."
Nuremberg officer. Pirkheimer was much inter-ested in military matters.

Page 21, line 5. "Club."
Literally "chamber," a Trinkhalle frequented by Pirkheimer. Apparently the habitués of the place had sent a chaffing message to Dürer, which he returns in kind by one pretending he had sent olive-wood to fumigate their meeting-place.

Page 21, line 29. "Doge."
Lorenzo Loredano, whose portrait by Giovanni Bellini is in the National Gallery, London.

Page 21, line 29. "Patriarch."
Either the Patriarch of Aquileja, or more prob-ably the Patriarch of Venice, who was a patron of S. Bartolommeo, for which the picture was destined.

Notes Page 22, line 2. "night."
1.00 a.m.

Page 22, line 7. "princes."
Or, "You would do better to correspond with princes."

To Letter IX

Page 22, line 16. "allegrezza."
Joy. In Venetian in original.

Page 22, line 18. "likewise."
Meaning doubtful.

Page 22, line 20. "quadro."
Painting. In Venetian in original. Perhaps the "Madonna" of the Berlin Gallery.

To Letter X

Page 24, line 13. "body."
Pirkheimer was thirty-six.

Page 24, line 16. "vostra."
Your. In Latin in original.

Page 25, line 9. "Luginsland."
A Nuremberg prison.

Page 25, last line. "Pender's."
A German inn-keeper.

Page 26, line 23. "Keppler."
A Nuremberg bookbinder.

Page 27, line 4. "lords."
The Town Councillors.

Page 27, line 11. "messenger."
He did not return till 1507.

To the Diary

Page 31, line 13. "Virgin," "Apocalypse."
This refers to the series of wood-engravings.

Page 31, line 20. "Hans."
Hans Wolf, court painter at Bamberg.

Page 37, line 23. "stivers."
A Netherlandish coin worth about 80 pfennigs.

Page 38, line 10. "three."
The third person was the maid Susanna.

Page 39, line 21. "Quentin's."
Quentin Matsys, the painter.

Page 39, line 23. "Staiber's."
Lorenz Staiber, a citizen of Nuremberg.

Page 40, line 3. "Charles."
Charles V.

Page 40, line 22. "Felix."
Felix Hungersberg. The drawing dated 1520 is in
the Albertina at Vienna.

Notes Page 41, line 5. "Joachim."
Joachim Patinir, the landscape painter.

Page 41, line 21. "Erasmus."
Erasmus of Rotterdam, the humanist.

Page 41, line 27. "Imagines."
The woodcuts known as imagines coeli.

Page 42, line 13. "Nicolas."
Nicolas Kratzer, whose portrait by Holbein is in
the Louvre.

Page 42, line 19. "Philip's."
A Netherlandish coin worth rather less than a
Rhenish florin.

Page 46, line 20. "Conrad."
Conrad Meyt, a Swiss sculptor.

Page 46, last line. "lords."
The Nuremberg Town Councillors, who were
bringing the insignia for the coronation of
Charles V.

Page 47, line 9. "Rogier."
Rogier van der Weyden.

Page 47, line 13. "Erasmus."
Not the great Erasmus, but a clerk in the service of Bannisis. The supplication has reference
to Dürer's claim for the continuance of his pension of 100 gulden, which was the main object
of his journey.

Page 47, line 22. "gold."
Mexico.

Page 48, line 13. "Nassau's."
Heinrich VIII, Statthalter of Holland.

Page 48, line 23. "Luke's."
Presumably an altar-piece supposed to have been painted by St. Luke.

Page 48, line 25. "Hugo."
Hugo van der Goes.

Page 49, line 5. "Bernhard."
Bernhard van Orley, court painter to the Grand Duchess Margaret.

Page 49, line 19. "Bernhard."
Probably a study for the portrait in the Dresden Gallery.

Page 49, line 26. "Eulenspiegels."
The popular "Till Eulenspiegel," which was printed at Augsburg, 1515.

Page 53, line 16. "Antwerp."
Probably the programme for Charles V's entry.

Page 53, line 29. "magistrates."
The giant's name was Brabo—the book is still at Antwerp.

Page 54, line 3. "Bologna."
Tommaso Vincidor, who came to the Netherlands on behalf of Leo X to see to the execution of some tapestries.

Notes Page 54, line 12. "sister."
A mistake of Dürer's; she was Charles V's aunt.

Page 54, line 27. "Dialogue."
Books relating to Luther's doctrines.

Page 55, line 8. "work."
That is, prints after Raphael.

Page 55, line 14. "crown."
Netherlandish coin worth 6.35 marks.

Page 56, line 3. "noble."
The Rosennobel = 8 marks, 20 pfennigs. The Flemish noble = 9 marks, 90 pfennigs.

Page 56, line 10. "Rome."
The pillars in the cathedral—they came from Theodoric's palace at Ravenna.

Page 56, line 19. "pf."
This was to make the silverpoint drawing of the cathedral now in the British Museum.

Page 56, line 22. "Mirror."
An inn of that name.

Page 56, line 27. "sketch-book."
These sketches are among the Holford drawings.

Page 57, line 11. "portrait."
This drawing is on the back of the sketch of Aachen.

Page 58, line 26. "pertele."
The word in the original is indecipherable.

Page 59, line 4. "Cologne."
The well-known altar-piece by Stephan Lochner in the cathedral at Cologne.

Page 59, last line. "Confirmation."
The confirmation by Charles V of the pension given by Maximilian.

Page 64, line 8. "Felix."
This portrait of Felix Hungersberg is in the Albertina.

Page 64, line 24. "headcloth."
A silverpoint drawing of Agnes Dürer in this headdress is in the Berlin Print Room.

Page 68, line 21. "head."
This can scarcely have been a picture; probably a drawing on a thin leaf of prepared wood, such as was used for sketch-books.

Page 70, line 25. "Knots."
Woodcuts imitating Leonardo da Vinci's device of a Knot.

Page 71, line 4. "Duke."
Frederick the Wise.

Page 71, line 14. "angel."
An English coin, equals 2 florins, 2 stivers, Netherlandish.

Page 72, line 13. "Bombelli's."
Which was designed by Dürer himself.

Notes Page 72, line 26. "Johann."
Jean Mane, a sculptor, afterwards employed by
Charles V.

Page 73, line 20. "Peter."
Peter Ægidius, the humanist.

Page 76, line 16. "Brussels."
Bernhard van Orley, whose portrait by Dürer is
in the Dresden Gallery.

Page 76, line 23. "wood."
Guaiac wood, used as a medicine.

Page 77, line 2. "silverpoint."
Now in the Uffizi.

Page 78, line 17. "Roger."
Rogier van der Weyden.

Page 78, line 17. "Hugo."
Hugo van der Goes.

Page 78, line 18. "alabaster."
More correctly marble. The statue is still in this
church.

Page 79, line 25. "Van Eyck's."
The great altar-piece of the "Adoration of the
Lamb," by Hubert and Jan Van Eyck, in St.
Baron's.

Page 81, line 12. "silverpoint."
This drawing is at Vienna.

Page 83, line 11. "Duke."
Probably of Frederick the Wise.

Page 83, line 22. "treacherously."
This was the usual idea at the time. He was really taken by the order of Frederick the Wise in order to protect him.

Page 85, line 17. "forty."
A reference to John Wycliffe.

Page 88, line 9. "Joachim."
Doubtless studies for Patinir to use in his landscapes.

Page 88, line 22. "Gerhardt."
Gerhardt Horebouts, who came afterwards with his daughter into the service of Henry VIII.

Page 90, line 29. "Margaret."
The Regent of the Netherlands.

Page 91, line 8. "Kaiser."
A painted portrait of the Emperor Maximilian.

Page 92, line 9. "Lucas."
Lucas van Leyden, the artist.

Page 92, line 15. "silverpoint."
In the Museum at Lille.

Page 94, line 27. "Lucas's."
Lucas van Leyden.

Notes Page 96, line 1. "Emperor."
The portrait of Maximilian, which was intended
for the Lady Margaret.

Page 96, line 17. "theriac."
An antidote for poison.

Page 98, line 1. "Spain."
Probably Eleanora of Portugal.

Page 98, line 3. "oils."
This picture no longer exists.

Page 99, line 12. "blanke."
A silver coin = 2 stivers.

A CATALOG OF SELECTED
DOVER BOOKS
IN ALL FIELDS OF INTEREST

A CATALOG OF SELECTED DOVER
BOOKS IN ALL FIELDS OF INTEREST

CONCERNING THE SPIRITUAL IN ART, Wassily Kandinsky. Pioneering work by father of abstract art. Thoughts on color theory, nature of art. Analysis of earlier masters. 12 illustrations. 80pp. of text. 5⅜ × 8½. 23411-8 Pa. $3.95

ANIMALS: 1,419 Copyright-Free Illustrations of Mammals, Birds, Fish, Insects, etc., Jim Harter (ed.). Clear wood engravings present, in extremely lifelike poses, over 1,000 species of animals. One of the most extensive pictorial sourcebooks of its kind. Captions. Index. 284pp. 9 × 12. 23766-4 Pa. $11.95

CELTIC ART: The Methods of Construction, George Bain. Simple geometric techniques for making Celtic interlacements, spirals, Kells-type initials, animals, humans, etc. Over 500 illustrations. 160pp. 9 × 12. (USO) 22923-8 Pa. $8.95

AN ATLAS OF ANATOMY FOR ARTISTS, Fritz Schider. Most thorough reference work on art anatomy in the world. Hundreds of illustrations, including selections from works by Vesalius, Leonardo, Goya, Ingres, Michelangelo, others. 593 illustrations. 192pp. 7⅛ × 10¼. 20241-0 Pa. $8.95

CELTIC HAND STROKE-BY-STROKE (Irish Half-Uncial from "The Book of Kells"): An Arthur Baker Calligraphy Manual, Arthur Baker. Complete guide to creating each letter of the alphabet in distinctive Celtic manner. Covers hand position, strokes, pens, inks, paper, more. Illustrated. 48pp. 8¼ × 11.
23336-2 Pa. $3.95

EASY ORIGAMI, John Montroll. Charming collection of 32 projects (hat, cup, pelican, piano, swan, many more) specially designed for the novice origami hobbyist. Clearly illustrated easy-to-follow instructions insure that even beginning papercrafters will achieve successful results. 48pp. 8¼ × 11. 27298-2 Pa. $2.95

THE COMPLETE BOOK OF BIRDHOUSE CONSTRUCTION FOR WOODWORKERS, Scott D. Campbell. Detailed instructions, illustrations, tables. Also data on bird habitat and instinct patterns. Bibliography. 3 tables. 63 illustrations in 15 figures. 48pp. 5¼ × 8½. 24407-5 Pa. $1.95

BLOOMINGDALE'S ILLUSTRATED 1886 CATALOG: Fashions, Dry Goods and Housewares, Bloomingdale Brothers. Famed merchants' extremely rare catalog depicting about 1,700 products: clothing, housewares, firearms, dry goods, jewelry, more. Invaluable for dating, identifying vintage items. Also, copyright-free graphics for artists, designers. Co-published with Henry Ford Museum & Greenfield Village. 160pp. 8¼ × 11. 25780-0 Pa. $9.95

HISTORIC COSTUME IN PICTURES, Braun & Schneider. Over 1,450 costumed figures in clearly detailed engravings—from dawn of civilization to end of 19th century. Captions. Many folk costumes. 256pp. 8⅜ × 11¾. 23150-X Pa. $10.95

STICKLEY CRAFTSMAN FURNITURE CATALOGS, Gustav Stickley and L. & J. G. Stickley. Beautiful, functional furniture in two authentic catalogs from 1910. 594 illustrations, including 277 photos, show settles, rockers, armchairs, reclining chairs, bookcases, desks, tables. 183pp. 6½ × 9¼. 23838-5 Pa. $8.95

AMERICAN LOCOMOTIVES IN HISTORIC PHOTOGRAPHS: 1858 to 1949, Ron Ziel (ed.). A rare collection of 126 meticulously detailed official photographs, called "builder portraits," of American locomotives that majestically chronicle the rise of steam locomotive power in America. Introduction. Detailed captions. xi + 129pp. 9 × 12. 27393-8 Pa. $12.95

AMERICA'S LIGHTHOUSES: An Illustrated History, Francis Ross Holland, Jr. Delightfully written, profusely illustrated fact-filled survey of over 200 American lighthouses since 1716. History, anecdotes, technological advances, more. 240pp. 8 × 10¾. 25576-X Pa. $11.95

TOWARDS A NEW ARCHITECTURE, Le Corbusier. Pioneering manifesto by founder of "International School." Technical and aesthetic theories, views of industry, economics, relation of form to function, "mass-production split" and much more. Profusely illustrated. 320pp. 6⅛ × 9¼. (USO) 25023-7 Pa. $8.95

HOW THE OTHER HALF LIVES, Jacob Riis. Famous journalistic record, exposing poverty and degradation of New York slums around 1900, by major social reformer. 100 striking and influential photographs. 233pp. 10 × 7⅞.
22012-5 Pa $10.95

FRUIT KEY AND TWIG KEY TO TREES AND SHRUBS, William M. Harlow. One of the handiest and most widely used identification aids. Fruit key covers 120 deciduous and evergreen species; twig key 160 deciduous species. Easily used. Over 300 photographs. 126pp. 5⅜ × 8½. 20511-8 Pa. $3.95

COMMON BIRD SONGS, Dr. Donald J. Borror. Songs of 60 most common U.S. birds: robins, sparrows, cardinals, bluejays, finches, more—arranged in order of increasing complexity. Up to 9 variations of songs of each species.
Cassette and manual 99911-4 $8.95

ORCHIDS AS HOUSE PLANTS, Rebecca Tyson Northen. Grow cattleyas and many other kinds of orchids—in a window, in a case, or under artificial light. 63 illustrations. 148pp. 5⅜ × 8½. 23261-1 Pa. $3.95

MONSTER MAZES, Dave Phillips. Masterful mazes at four levels of difficulty. Avoid deadly perils and evil creatures to find magical treasures. Solutions for all 32 exciting illustrated puzzles. 48pp. 8¼ × 11. 26005-4 Pa. $2.95

MOZART'S DON GIOVANNI (DOVER OPERA LIBRETTO SERIES), Wolfgang Amadeus Mozart. Introduced and translated by Ellen H. Bleiler. Standard Italian libretto, with complete English translation. Convenient and thoroughly portable—an ideal companion for reading along with a recording or the performance itself. Introduction. List of characters. Plot summary. 121pp. 5¼ × 8½.
24944-1 Pa. $2.95

TECHNICAL MANUAL AND DICTIONARY OF CLASSICAL BALLET, Gail Grant. Defines, explains, comments on steps, movements, poses and concepts. 15-page pictorial section. Basic book for student, viewer. 127pp. 5⅜ × 8½.
21843-0 Pa. $3.95

BRASS INSTRUMENTS: Their History and Development, Anthony Baines. Authoritative, updated survey of the evolution of trumpets, trombones, bugles, cornets, French horns, tubas and other brass wind instruments. Over 140 illustrations and 48 music examples. Corrected and updated by author. New preface. Bibliography. 320pp. 5⅜ × 8½. 27574-4 Pa. $9.95

HOLLYWOOD GLAMOR PORTRAITS, John Kobal (ed.). 145 photos from 1926–49. Harlow, Gable, Bogart, Bacall; 94 stars in all. Full background on photographers, technical aspects. 160pp. 8⅜ × 11¼. 23352-9 Pa. $9.95

MAX AND MORITZ, Wilhelm Busch. Great humor classic in both German and English. Also 10 other works: "Cat and Mouse," "Plisch and Plumm," etc. 216pp. 5⅜ × 8½. 20181-3 Pa. $5.95

THE RAVEN AND OTHER FAVORITE POEMS, Edgar Allan Poe. Over 40 of the author's most memorable poems: "The Bells," "Ulalume," "Israfel," "To Helen," "The Conqueror Worm," "Eldorado," "Annabel Lee," many more. Alphabetic lists of titles and first lines. 64pp. 5$^{3}/_{16}$ × 8¼. 26685-0 Pa. $1.00

SEVEN SCIENCE FICTION NOVELS, H. G. Wells. The standard collection of the great novels. Complete, unabridged. First Men in the Moon, Island of Dr. Moreau, War of the Worlds, Food of the Gods, Invisible Man, Time Machine, In the Days of the Comet. Total of 1,015pp. 5⅜ × 8½. (USO) 20264-X Clothbd. $29.95

AMULETS AND SUPERSTITIONS, E. A. Wallis Budge. Comprehensive discourse on origin, powers of amulets in many ancient cultures: Arab, Persian, Babylonian, Assyrian, Egyptian, Gnostic, Hebrew, Phoenician, Syriac, etc. Covers cross, swastika, crucifix, seals, rings, stones, etc. 584pp. 5⅜ × 8½. 23573-4 Pa. $12.95

RUSSIAN STORIES/PYCCKNE PACCKA3bl: A Dual-Language Book, edited by Gleb Struve. Twelve tales by such masters as Chekhov, Tolstoy, Dostoevsky, Pushkin, others. Excellent word-for-word English translations on facing pages, plus teaching and study aids, Russian/English vocabulary, biographical/critical introductions, more. 416pp. 5⅜ × 8½. 26244-8 Pa. $8.95

PHILADELPHIA THEN AND NOW: 60 Sites Photographed in the Past and Present, Kenneth Finkel and Susan Oyama. Rare photographs of City Hall, Logan Square, Independence Hall, Betsy Ross House, other landmarks juxtaposed with contemporary views. Captures changing face of historic city. Introduction. Captions. 128pp. 8¼ × 11. 25790-8 Pa. $9.95

AIA ARCHITECTURAL GUIDE TO NASSAU AND SUFFOLK COUNTIES, LONG ISLAND, The American Institute of Architects, Long Island Chapter, and the Society for the Preservation of Long Island Antiquities. Comprehensive, well-researched and generously illustrated volume brings to life over three centuries of Long Island's great architectural heritage. More than 240 photographs with authoritative, extensively detailed captions. 176pp. 8¼ × 11. 26946-9 Pa. $14.95

NORTH AMERICAN INDIAN LIFE: Customs and Traditions of 23 Tribes, Elsie Clews Parsons (ed.). 27 fictionalized essays by noted anthropologists examine religion, customs, government, additional facets of life among the Winnebago, Crow, Zuni, Eskimo, other tribes. 480pp. 6⅛ × 9¼. 27377-6 Pa. $10.95

FRANK LLOYD WRIGHT'S HOLLYHOCK HOUSE, Donald Hoffmann. Lavishly illustrated, carefully documented study of one of Wright's most controversial residential designs. Over 120 photographs, floor plans, elevations, etc. Detailed perceptive text by noted Wright scholar. Index. 128pp. 9¼ × 10¾.
27133-1 Pa. $11.95

THE MALE AND FEMALE FIGURE IN MOTION: 60 Classic Photographic Sequences, Eadweard Muybridge. 60 true-action photographs of men and women walking, running, climbing, bending, turning, etc., reproduced from rare 19th-century masterpiece. vi + 121pp. 9 × 12. 24745-7 Pa. $10.95

1001 QUESTIONS ANSWERED ABOUT THE SEASHORE, N. J. Berrill and Jacquelyn Berrill. Queries answered about dolphins, sea snails, sponges, starfish, fishes, shore birds, many others. Covers appearance, breeding, growth, feeding, much more. 305pp. 5¼ × 8¼. 23366-9 Pa. $7.95

GUIDE TO OWL WATCHING IN NORTH AMERICA, Donald S. Heintzelman. Superb guide offers complete data and descriptions of 19 species: barn owl, screech owl, snowy owl, many more. Expert coverage of owl-watching equipment, conservation, migrations and invasions, etc. Guide to observing sites. 84 illustrations. xiii + 193pp. 5⅜ × 8½. 27344-X Pa. $7.95

MEDICINAL AND OTHER USES OF NORTH AMERICAN PLANTS: A Historical Survey with Special Reference to the Eastern Indian Tribes, Charlotte Erichsen-Brown. Chronological historical citations document 500 years of usage of plants, trees, shrubs native to eastern Canada, northeastern U.S. Also complete identifying information. 343 illustrations. 544pp. 6½ × 9¼. 25951-X Pa. $12.95

STORYBOOK MAZES, Dave Phillips. 23 stories and mazes on two-page spreads: Wizard of Oz, Treasure Island, Robin Hood, etc. Solutions. 64pp. 8¼ × 11.
23628-5 Pa. $2.95

NEGRO FOLK MUSIC, U.S.A., Harold Courlander. Noted folklorist's scholarly yet readable analysis of rich and varied musical tradition. Includes authentic versions of over 40 folk songs. Valuable bibliography and discography. xi + 324pp. 5⅜ × 8½. 27350-4 Pa. $7.95

MOVIE-STAR PORTRAITS OF THE FORTIES, John Kobal (ed.). 163 glamor, studio photos of 106 stars of the 1940s: Rita Hayworth, Ava Gardner, Marlon Brando, Clark Gable, many more. 176pp. 8⅜ × 11¼. 23546-7 Pa. $10.95

BENCHLEY LOST AND FOUND, Robert Benchley. Finest humor from early 30s, about pet peeves, child psychologists, post office and others. Mostly unavailable elsewhere. 73 illustrations by Peter Arno and others. 183pp. 5⅜ × 8½.
22410-4 Pa. $5.95

YEKL and THE IMPORTED BRIDEGROOM AND OTHER STORIES OF YIDDISH NEW YORK, Abraham Cahan. Film Hester Street based on Yekl (1896). Novel, other stories among first about Jewish immigrants on N.Y.'s East Side. 240pp. 5⅜ × 8½. 22427-9 Pa. $5.95

SELECTED POEMS, Walt Whitman. Generous sampling from Leaves of Grass. Twenty-four poems include "I Hear America Singing," "Song of the Open Road," "I Sing the Body Electric," "When Lilacs Last in the Dooryard Bloom'd," "O Captain! My Captain!"—all reprinted from an authoritative edition. Lists of titles and first lines. 128pp. 5³⁄₁₆ × 8¼. 26878-0 Pa. $1.00

THE BEST TALES OF HOFFMANN, E. T. A. Hoffmann. 10 of Hoffmann's most important stories: "Nutcracker and the King of Mice," "The Golden Flowerpot," etc. 458pp. 5⅜ × 8½. 21793-0 Pa. $8.95

FROM FETISH TO GOD IN ANCIENT EGYPT, E. A. Wallis Budge. Rich detailed survey of Egyptian conception of "God" and gods, magic, cult of animals, Osiris, more. Also, superb English translations of hymns and legends. 240 illustrations. 545pp. 5⅜ × 8½. 25803-3 Pa. $11.95

FRENCH STORIES/CONTES FRANÇAIS: A Dual-Language Book, Wallace Fowlie. Ten stories by French masters, Voltaire to Camus: "Micromegas" by Voltaire; "The Atheist's Mass" by Balzac; "Minuet" by de Maupassant; "The Guest" by Camus, six more. Excellent English translations on facing pages. Also French-English vocabulary list, exercises, more. 352pp. 5⅜ × 8½. 26443-2 Pa. $8.95

CHICAGO AT THE TURN OF THE CENTURY IN PHOTOGRAPHS: 122 Historic Views from the Collections of the Chicago Historical Society, Larry A. Viskochil. Rare large-format prints offer detailed views of City Hall, State Street, the Loop, Hull House, Union Station, many other landmarks, circa 1904–1913. Introduction. Captions. Maps. 144pp. 9⅜ × 12¼. 24656-6 Pa. $12.95

OLD BROOKLYN IN EARLY PHOTOGRAPHS, 1865–1929, William Lee Younger. Luna Park, Gravesend race track, construction of Grand Army Plaza, moving of Hotel Brighton, etc. 157 previously unpublished photographs. 165pp. 8⅞ × 11¾. 23587-4 Pa. $12.95

THE MYTHS OF THE NORTH AMERICAN INDIANS, Lewis Spence. Rich anthology of the myths and legends of the Algonquins, Iroquois, Pawnees and Sioux, prefaced by an extensive historical and ethnological commentary. 36 illustrations. 480pp. 5⅜ × 8½. 25967-6 Pa. $8.95

AN ENCYCLOPEDIA OF BATTLES: Accounts of Over 1,560 Battles from 1479 B.C. to the Present, David Eggenberger. Essential details of every major battle in recorded history from the first battle of Megiddo in 1479 B.C. to Grenada in 1984. List of Battle Maps. New Appendix covering the years 1967–1984. Index. 99 illustrations. 544pp. 6½ × 9¼. 24913-1 Pa. $14.95

SAILING ALONE AROUND THE WORLD, Captain Joshua Slocum. First man to sail around the world, alone, in small boat. One of great feats of seamanship told in delightful manner. 67 illustrations. 294pp. 5⅜ × 8½. 20326-3 Pa. $5.95

ANARCHISM AND OTHER ESSAYS, Emma Goldman. Powerful, penetrating, prophetic essays on direct action, role of minorities, prison reform, puritan hypocrisy, violence, etc. 271pp. 5⅜ × 8½. 22484-8 Pa. $5.95

MYTHS OF THE HINDUS AND BUDDHISTS, Ananda K. Coomaraswamy and Sister Nivedita. Great stories of the epics; deeds of Krishna, Shiva, taken from puranas, Vedas, folk tales; etc. 32 illustrations. 400pp. 5⅜ × 8½. 21759-0 Pa. $9.95

BEYOND PSYCHOLOGY, Otto Rank. Fear of death, desire of immortality, nature of sexuality, social organization, creativity, according to Rankian system. 291pp. 5⅜ × 8½. 20485-5 Pa. $7.95

A THEOLOGICO-POLITICAL TREATISE, Benedict Spinoza. Also contains unfinished Political Treatise. Great classic on religious liberty, theory of government on common consent. R. Elwes translation. Total of 421pp. 5⅜ × 8½. 20249-6 Pa. $7.95

MY BONDAGE AND MY FREEDOM, Frederick Douglass. Born a slave, Douglass became outspoken force in antislavery movement. The best of Douglass' autobiographies. Graphic description of slave life. 464pp. 5⅜ × 8½.   22457-0 Pa. $8.95

FOLLOWING THE EQUATOR: A Journey Around the World, Mark Twain. Fascinating humorous account of 1897 voyage to Hawaii, Australia, India, New Zealand, etc. Ironic, bemused reports on peoples, customs, climate, flora and fauna, politics, much more. 197 illustrations. 720pp. 5⅜ × 8½.   26113-1 Pa. $15.95

THE PEOPLE CALLED SHAKERS, Edward D. Andrews. Definitive study of Shakers: origins, beliefs, practices, dances, social organization, furniture and crafts, etc. 33 illustrations. 351pp. 5⅜ × 8½.   21081-2 Pa. $7.95

THE MYTHS OF GREECE AND ROME, H. A. Guerber. A classic of mythology, generously illustrated, long prized for its simple, graphic, accurate retelling of the principal myths of Greece and Rome, and for its commentary on their origins and significance. With 64 illustrations by Michelangelo, Raphael, Titian, Rubens, Canova, Bernini and others. 480pp. 5⅜ × 8½.   27584-1 Pa. $9.95

PSYCHOLOGY OF MUSIC, Carl E. Seashore. Classic work discusses music as a medium from psychological viewpoint. Clear treatment of physical acoustics, auditory apparatus, sound perception, development of musical skills, nature of musical feeling, host of other topics. 88 figures. 408pp. 5⅜ × 8½. 21851-1 Pa. $9.95

THE PHILOSOPHY OF HISTORY, Georg W. Hegel. Great classic of Western thought develops concept that history is not chance but rational process, the evolution of freedom. 457pp. 5⅜ × 8½.   20112-0 Pa. $8.95

THE BOOK OF TEA, Kakuzo Okakura. Minor classic of the Orient: entertaining, charming explanation, interpretation of traditional Japanese culture in terms of tea ceremony. 94pp. 5⅜ × 8½.   20070-1 Pa. $2.95

LIFE IN ANCIENT EGYPT, Adolf Erman. Fullest, most thorough, detailed older account with much not in more recent books, domestic life, religion, magic, medicine, commerce, much more. Many illustrations reproduce tomb paintings, carvings, hieroglyphs, etc. 597pp. 5⅜ × 8½.   22632-8 Pa. $9.95

SUNDIALS, Their Theory and Construction, Albert Waugh. Far and away the best, most thorough coverage of ideas, mathematics concerned, types, construction, adjusting anywhere. Simple, nontechnical treatment allows even children to build several of these dials. Over 100 illustrations. 230pp. 5⅜ × 8½.   22947-5 Pa. $5.95

DYNAMICS OF FLUIDS IN POROUS MEDIA, Jacob Bear. For advanced students of ground water hydrology, soil mechanics and physics, drainage and irrigation engineering, and more. 335 illustrations. Exercises, with answers. 784pp. 6⅛ × 9¼.   65675-6 Pa. $19.95

SONGS OF EXPERIENCE: Facsimile Reproduction with 26 Plates in Full Color, William Blake. 26 full-color plates from a rare 1826 edition. Includes "The Tyger," "London," "Holy Thursday," and other poems. Printed text of poems. 48pp. 5¼ × 7.   24636-1 Pa. $3.95

OLD-TIME VIGNETTES IN FULL COLOR, Carol Belanger Grafton (ed.). Over 390 charming, often sentimental illustrations, selected from archives of Victorian graphics—pretty women posing, children playing, food, flowers, kittens and puppies, smiling cherubs, birds and butterflies, much more. All copyright-free. 48pp. 9¼ × 12¼.   27269-9 Pa. $5.95

CATALOG OF DOVER BOOKS

PERSPECTIVE FOR ARTISTS, Rex Vicat Cole. Depth, perspective of sky and sea, shadows, much more, not usually covered. 391 diagrams, 81 reproductions of drawings and paintings. 279pp. 5⅜ × 8½. 22487-2 Pa. $6.95

DRAWING THE LIVING FIGURE, Joseph Sheppard. Innovative approach to artistic anatomy focuses on specifics of surface anatomy, rather than muscles and bones. Over 170 drawings of live models in front, back and side views, and in widely varying poses. Accompanying diagrams. 177 illustrations. Introduction. Index. 144pp. 8⅜ × 11¼. 26723-7 Pa. $7.95

GOTHIC AND OLD ENGLISH ALPHABETS: 100 Complete Fonts, Dan X. Solo. Add power, elegance to posters, signs, other graphics with 100 stunning copyright-free alphabets: Blackstone, Dolbey, Germania, 97 more—including many lower-case, numerals, punctuation marks. 104pp. 8⅛ × 11. 24695-7 Pa. $7.95

HOW TO DO BEADWORK, Mary White. Fundamental book on craft from simple projects to five-bead chains and woven works. 106 illustrations. 142pp. 5⅜ × 8. 20697-1 Pa. $4.95

THE BOOK OF WOOD CARVING, Charles Marshall Sayers. Finest book for beginners discusses fundamentals and offers 34 designs. "Absolutely first rate . . . well thought out and well executed."—E. J. Tangerman. 118pp. 7¾ × 10⅝. 23654-4 Pa. $5.95

ILLUSTRATED CATALOG OF CIVIL WAR MILITARY GOODS: Union Army Weapons, Insignia, Uniform Accessories, and Other Equipment, Schuyler, Hartley, and Graham. Rare, profusely illustrated 1846 catalog includes Union Army uniform and dress regulations, arms and ammunition, coats, insignia, flags, swords, rifles, etc. 226 illustrations. 160pp. 9 × 12. 24939-5 Pa. $10.95

WOMEN'S FASHIONS OF THE EARLY 1900s: An Unabridged Republication of "New York Fashions, 1909," National Cloak & Suit Co. Rare catalog of mail-order fashions documents women's and children's clothing styles shortly after the turn of the century. Captions offer full descriptions, prices. Invaluable resource for fashion, costume historians. Approximately 725 illustrations. 128pp. 8⅜ × 11¼. 27276-1 Pa. $10.95

THE 1912 AND 1915 GUSTAV STICKLEY FURNITURE CATALOGS, Gustav Stickley. With over 200 detailed illustrations and descriptions, these two catalogs are essential reading and reference materials and identification guides for Stickley furniture. Captions cite materials, dimensions and prices. 112pp. 6½ × 9¼. 26676-1 Pa. $9.95

EARLY AMERICAN LOCOMOTIVES, John H. White, Jr. Finest locomotive engravings from early 19th century: historical (1804–74), main-line (after 1870), special, foreign, etc. 147 plates. 142pp. 11⅜ × 8¼. 22772-3 Pa. $8.95

THE TALL SHIPS OF TODAY IN PHOTOGRAPHS, Frank O. Braynard. Lavishly illustrated tribute to nearly 100 majestic contemporary sailing vessels: Amerigo Vespucci, Clearwater, Constitution, Eagle, Mayflower, Sea Cloud, Victory, many more. Authoritative captions provide statistics, background on each ship. 190 black-and-white photographs and illustrations. Introduction. 128pp. 8⅞ × 11¾. 27163-3 Pa. $12.95

EARLY NINETEENTH-CENTURY CRAFTS AND TRADES, Peter Stockham (ed.). Extremely rare 1807 volume describes to youngsters the crafts and trades of the day: brickmaker, weaver, dressmaker, bookbinder, ropemaker, saddler, many more. Quaint prose, charming illustrations for each craft. 20 black-and-white line illustrations. 192pp. 4⅝ × 6.   27293-1 Pa. $4.95

VICTORIAN FASHIONS AND COSTUMES FROM HARPER'S BAZAR, 1867–1898, Stella Blum (ed.). Day costumes, evening wear, sports clothes, shoes, hats, other accessories in over 1,000 detailed engravings. 320pp. 9⅜ × 12¼.
22990-4 Pa. $13.95

GUSTAV STICKLEY, THE CRAFTSMAN, Mary Ann Smith. Superb study surveys broad scope of Stickley's achievement, especially in architecture. Design philosophy, rise and fall of the Craftsman empire, descriptions and floor plans for many Craftsman houses, more. 86 black-and-white halftones. 31 line illustrations. Introduction. 208pp. 6½ × 9¼.   27210-9 Pa. $9.95

THE LONG ISLAND RAIL ROAD IN EARLY PHOTOGRAPHS, Ron Ziel. Over 220 rare photos, informative text document origin (1844) and development of rail service on Long Island. Vintage views of early trains, locomotives, stations, passengers, crews, much more. Captions. 8⅞ × 11¾.   26301-0 Pa. $13.95

THE BOOK OF OLD SHIPS: From Egyptian Galleys to Clipper Ships, Henry B. Culver. Superb, authoritative history of sailing vessels, with 80 magnificent line illustrations. Galley, bark, caravel, longship, whaler, many more. Detailed, informative text on each vessel by noted naval historian. Introduction. 256pp. 5⅜ × 8½.   27332-6 Pa. $6.95

TEN BOOKS ON ARCHITECTURE, Vitruvius. The most important book ever written on architecture. Early Roman aesthetics, technology, classical orders, site selection, all other aspects. Morgan translation. 331pp. 5⅜ × 8½. 20645-9 Pa. $8.95

THE HUMAN FIGURE IN MOTION, Eadweard Muybridge. More than 4,500 stopped-action photos, in action series, showing undraped men, women, children jumping, lying down, throwing, sitting, wrestling, carrying, etc. 390pp. 7⅞ × 10⅝.
20204-6 Clothbd. $24.95

TREES OF THE EASTERN AND CENTRAL UNITED STATES AND CANADA, William M. Harlow. Best one-volume guide to 140 trees. Full descriptions, woodlore, range, etc. Over 600 illustrations. Handy size. 288pp. 4½ × 6⅜.
20395-6 Pa. $5.95

SONGS OF WESTERN BIRDS, Dr. Donald J. Borror. Complete song and call repertoire of 60 western species, including flycatchers, juncoes, cactus wrens, many more—includes fully illustrated booklet.   Cassette and manual 99913-0 $8.95

GROWING AND USING HERBS AND SPICES, Milo Miloradovich. Versatile handbook provides all the information needed for cultivation and use of all the herbs and spices available in North America. 4 illustrations. Index. Glossary. 236pp. 5⅜ × 8½.   25058-X Pa. $5.95

BIG BOOK OF MAZES AND LABYRINTHS, Walter Shepherd. 50 mazes and labyrinths in all—classical, solid, ripple, and more—in one great volume. Perfect inexpensive puzzler for clever youngsters. Full solutions. 112pp. 8⅛ × 11.
22951-3 Pa. $3.95

PIANO TUNING, J. Cree Fischer. Clearest, best book for beginner, amateur. Simple repairs, raising dropped notes, tuning by easy method of flattened fifths. No previous skills needed. 4 illustrations. 201pp. 5⅜ × 8½. 23267-0 Pa. $5.95

A SOURCE BOOK IN THEATRICAL HISTORY, A. M. Nagler. Contemporary observers on acting, directing, make-up, costuming, stage props, machinery, scene design, from Ancient Greece to Chekhov. 611pp. 5⅜ × 8½. 20515-0 Pa. $11.95

THE COMPLETE NONSENSE OF EDWARD LEAR, Edward Lear. All nonsense limericks, zany alphabets, Owl and Pussycat, songs, nonsense botany, etc., illustrated by Lear. Total of 320pp. 5⅜ × 8½. (USO) 20167-8 Pa. $5.95

VICTORIAN PARLOUR POETRY: An Annotated Anthology, Michael R. Turner. 117 gems by Longfellow, Tennyson, Browning, many lesser-known poets. "The Village Blacksmith," "Curfew Must Not Ring Tonight," "Only a Baby Small," dozens more, often difficult to find elsewhere. Index of poets, titles, first lines. xxiii + 325pp. 5⅜ × 8¼. 27044-0 Pa. $8.95

DUBLINERS, James Joyce. Fifteen stories offer vivid, tightly focused observations of the lives of Dublin's poorer classes. At least one, "The Dead," is considered a masterpiece. Reprinted complete and unabridged from standard edition. 160pp. 5³⁄₁₆ × 8¼. 26870-5 Pa. $1.00

THE HAUNTED MONASTERY and THE CHINESE MAZE MURDERS, Robert van Gulik. Two full novels by van Gulik, set in 7th-century China, continue adventures of Judge Dee and his companions. An evil Taoist monastery, seemingly supernatural events; overgrown topiary maze hides strange crimes. 27 illustrations. 328pp. 5⅜ × 8½. 23502-5 Pa. $7.95

THE BOOK OF THE SACRED MAGIC OF ABRAMELIN THE MAGE, translated by S. MacGregor Mathers. Medieval manuscript of ceremonial magic. Basic document in Aleister Crowley, Golden Dawn groups. 268pp. 5⅜ × 8½. 23211-5 Pa. $7.95

NEW RUSSIAN-ENGLISH AND ENGLISH-RUSSIAN DICTIONARY, M. A. O'Brien. This is a remarkably handy Russian dictionary, containing a surprising amount of information, including over 70,000 entries. 366pp. 4½ × 6⅛. 20208-9 Pa. $8.95

HISTORIC HOMES OF THE AMERICAN PRESIDENTS, Second, Revised Edition, Irvin Haas. A traveler's guide to American Presidential homes, most open to the public, depicting and describing homes occupied by every American President from George Washington to George Bush. With visiting hours, admission charges, travel routes. 175 photographs. Index. 160pp. 8¼ × 11. 26751-2 Pa. $10.95

NEW YORK IN THE FORTIES, Andreas Feininger. 162 brilliant photographs by the well-known photographer, formerly with *Life* magazine. Commuters, shoppers, Times Square at night, much else from city at its peak. Captions by John von Hartz. 181pp. 9¼ × 10¾. 23585-8 Pa. $12.95

INDIAN SIGN LANGUAGE, William Tomkins. Over 525 signs developed by Sioux and other tribes. Written instructions and diagrams. Also 290 pictographs. 111pp. 6⅛ × 9¼. 22029-X Pa. $3.50

ANATOMY: A Complete Guide for Artists, Joseph Sheppard. A master of figure drawing shows artists how to render human anatomy convincingly. Over 460 illustrations. 224pp. 8⅜ × 11¼. 27279-6 Pa. $9.95

MEDIEVAL CALLIGRAPHY: Its History and Technique, Marc Drogin. Spirited history, comprehensive instruction manual covers 13 styles (ca. 4th century thru 15th). Excellent photographs; directions for duplicating medieval techniques with modern tools. 224pp. 8⅜ × 11¼. 26142-5 Pa. $11.95

DRIED FLOWERS: How to Prepare Them, Sarah Whitlock and Martha Rankin. Complete instructions on how to use silica gel, meal and borax, perlite aggregate, sand and borax, glycerine and water to create attractive permanent flower arrangements. 12 illustrations. 32pp. 5⅜ × 8½. 21802-3 Pa. $1.00

EASY-TO-MAKE BIRD FEEDERS FOR WOODWORKERS, Scott D. Campbell. Detailed, simple-to-use guide for designing, constructing, caring for and using feeders. Text, illustrations for 12 classic and contemporary designs. 96pp. 5⅜ × 8½. 25847-5 Pa. $2.95

OLD-TIME CRAFTS AND TRADES, Peter Stockham. An 1807 book created to teach children about crafts and trades open to them as future careers. It describes in detailed, nontechnical terms 24 different occupations, among them coachmaker, gardener, hairdresser, lacemaker, shoemaker, wheelwright, copper-plate printer, milliner, trunkmaker, merchant and brewer. Finely detailed engravings illustrate each occupation. 192pp. 4⅜ × 6. 27398-9 Pa. $4.95

THE HISTORY OF UNDERCLOTHES, C. Willett Cunnington and Phyllis Cunnington. Fascinating, well-documented survey covering six centuries of English undergarments, enhanced with over 100 illustrations: 12th-century laced-up bodice, footed long drawers (1795), 19th-century bustles, 19th-century corsets for men, Victorian "bust improvers," much more. 272pp. 5⅜ × 8¼. 27124-2 Pa. $9.95

ARTS AND CRAFTS FURNITURE: The Complete Brooks Catalog of 1912, Brooks Manufacturing Co. Photos and detailed descriptions of more than 150 now very collectible furniture designs from the Arts and Crafts movement depict davenports, settees, buffets, desks, tables, chairs, bedsteads, dressers and more, all built of solid, quarter-sawed oak. Invaluable for students and enthusiasts of antiques, Americana and the decorative arts. 80pp. 6½ × 9¼. 27471-3 Pa. $7.95

HOW WE INVENTED THE AIRPLANE: An Illustrated History, Orville Wright. Fascinating firsthand account covers early experiments, construction of planes and motors, first flights, much more. Introduction and commentary by Fred C. Kelly. 76 photographs. 96pp. 8¼ × 11. 25662-6 Pa. $7.95

THE ARTS OF THE SAILOR: Knotting, Splicing and Ropework, Hervey Garrett Smith. Indispensable shipboard reference covers tools, basic knots and useful hitches; handsewing and canvas work, more. Over 100 illustrations. Delightful reading for sea lovers. 256pp. 5⅜ × 8½. 26440-8 Pa. $7.95

FRANK LLOYD WRIGHT'S FALLINGWATER: The House and Its History, Second, Revised Edition, Donald Hoffmann. A total revision—both in text and illustrations—of the standard document on Fallingwater, the boldest, most personal architectural statement of Wright's mature years, updated with valuable new material from the recently opened Frank Lloyd Wright Archives. "Fascinating"—*The New York Times.* 116 illustrations. 128pp. 9¼ × 10¾. 27430-6 Pa. $10.95

PHOTOGRAPHIC SKETCHBOOK OF THE CIVIL WAR, Alexander Gardner. 100 photos taken on field during the Civil War. Famous shots of Manassas, Harper's Ferry, Lincoln, Richmond, slave pens, etc. 244pp. 10⅝ × 8¼.
22731-6 Pa. $9.95

FIVE ACRES AND INDEPENDENCE, Maurice G. Kains. Great back-to-the-land classic explains basics of self-sufficient farming. The one book to get. 95 illustrations. 397pp. 5⅜ × 8½.
20974-1 Pa. $6.95

SONGS OF EASTERN BIRDS, Dr. Donald J. Borror. Songs and calls of 60 species most common to eastern U.S.: warblers, woodpeckers, flycatchers, thrushes, larks, many more in high-quality recording.
Cassette and manual 99912-2 $8.95

A MODERN HERBAL, Margaret Grieve. Much the fullest, most exact, most useful compilation of herbal material. Gigantic alphabetical encyclopedia, from aconite to zedoary, gives botanical information, medical properties, folklore, economic uses, much else. Indispensable to serious reader. 161 illustrations. 888pp. 6½ × 9¼. 2-vol. set. (USO)
Vol. I: 22798-7 Pa. $9.95
Vol. II: 22799-5 Pa. $9.95

HIDDEN TREASURE MAZE BOOK, Dave Phillips. Solve 34 challenging mazes accompanied by heroic tales of adventure. Evil dragons, people-eating plants, bloodthirsty giants, many more dangerous adversaries lurk at every twist and turn. 34 mazes, stories, solutions. 48pp. 8¼ × 11.
24566-7 Pa. $2.95

LETTERS OF W. A. MOZART, Wolfgang A. Mozart. Remarkable letters show bawdy wit, humor, imagination, musical insights, contemporary musical world; includes some letters from Leopold Mozart. 276pp. 5⅜ × 8½.
22859-2 Pa. $6.95

BASIC PRINCIPLES OF CLASSICAL BALLET, Agrippina Vaganova. Great Russian theoretician, teacher explains methods for teaching classical ballet. 118 illustrations. 175pp. 5⅜ × 8½.
22036-2 Pa. $4.95

THE JUMPING FROG, Mark Twain. Revenge edition. The original story of The Celebrated Jumping Frog of Calaveras County, a hapless French translation, and Twain's hilarious "retranslation" from the French. 12 illustrations. 66pp. 5⅜ × 8½.
22686-7 Pa. $3.50

BEST REMEMBERED POEMS, Martin Gardner (ed.). The 126 poems in this superb collection of 19th- and 20th-century British and American verse range from Shelley's "To a Skylark" to the impassioned "Renascence" of Edna St. Vincent Millay and to Edward Lear's whimsical "The Owl and the Pussycat." 224pp. 5⅜ × 8½.
27165-X Pa. $4.95

COMPLETE SONNETS, William Shakespeare. Over 150 exquisite poems deal with love, friendship, the tyranny of time, beauty's evanescence, death and other themes in language of remarkable power, precision and beauty. Glossary of archaic terms. 80pp. 5³⁄₁₆ × 8¼.
26686-9 Pa. $1.00

BODIES IN A BOOKSHOP, R. T. Campbell. Challenging mystery of blackmail and murder with ingenious plot and superbly drawn characters. In the best tradition of British suspense fiction. 192pp. 5⅜ × 8½.
24720-1 Pa. $5.95

THE WIT AND HUMOR OF OSCAR WILDE, Alvin Redman (ed.). More than 1,000 ripostes, paradoxes, wisecracks: Work is the curse of the drinking classes; I can resist everything except temptation; etc. 258pp. 5⅜ × 8½. 20602-5 Pa. $4.95

SHAKESPEARE LEXICON AND QUOTATION DICTIONARY, Alexander Schmidt. Full definitions, locations, shades of meaning in every word in plays and poems. More than 50,000 exact quotations. 1,485pp. 6½ × 9¼. 2-vol. set.
Vol. 1: 22726-X Pa. $15.95
Vol. 2: 22727-8 Pa. $15.95

SELECTED POEMS, Emily Dickinson. Over 100 best-known, best-loved poems by one of America's foremost poets, reprinted from authoritative early editions. No comparable edition at this price. Index of first lines. 64pp. 5³⁄₁₆ × 8¼.
26466-1 Pa. $1.00

CELEBRATED CASES OF JUDGE DEE (DEE GOONG AN), translated by Robert van Gulik. Authentic 18th-century Chinese detective novel; Dee and associates solve three interlocked cases. Led to van Gulik's own stories with same characters. Extensive introduction. 9 illustrations. 237pp. 5⅜ × 8½.
23337-5 Pa. $5.95

THE MALLEUS MALEFICARUM OF KRAMER AND SPRENGER, translated by Montague Summers. Full text of most important witchhunter's "bible," used by both Catholics and Protestants. 278pp. 6⅝ × 10. 22802-9 Pa. $10.95

SPANISH STORIES/CUENTOS ESPAÑOLES: A Dual-Language Book, Angel Flores (ed.). Unique format offers 13 great stories in Spanish by Cervantes, Borges, others. Faithful English translations on facing pages. 352pp. 5⅜ × 8½.
25399-6 Pa. $8.95

THE CHICAGO WORLD'S FAIR OF 1893: A Photographic Record, Stanley Appelbaum (ed.). 128 rare photos show 200 buildings, Beaux-Arts architecture, Midway, original Ferris Wheel, Edison's kinetoscope, more. Architectural emphasis; full text. 116pp. 8¼ × 11. 23990-X Pa. $9.95

OLD QUEENS, N.Y., IN EARLY PHOTOGRAPHS, Vincent F. Seyfried and William Asadorian. Over 160 rare photographs of Maspeth, Jamaica, Jackson Heights, and other areas. Vintage views of DeWitt Clinton mansion, 1939 World's Fair and more. Captions. 192pp. 8⅞ × 11. 26358-4 Pa. $12.95

CAPTURED BY THE INDIANS: 15 Firsthand Accounts, 1750–1870, Frederick Drimmer. Astounding true historical accounts of grisly torture, bloody conflicts, relentless pursuits, miraculous escapes and more, by people who lived to tell the tale. 384pp. 5⅜ × 8½. 24901-8 Pa. $7.95

THE WORLD'S GREAT SPEECHES, Lewis Copeland and Lawrence W. Lamm (eds.). Vast collection of 278 speeches of Greeks to 1970. Powerful and effective models; unique look at history. 842pp. 5⅜ × 8½. 20468-5 Pa. $13.95

THE BOOK OF THE SWORD, Sir Richard F. Burton. Great Victorian scholar/adventurer's eloquent, erudite history of the "queen of weapons"—from prehistory to early Roman Empire. Evolution and development of early swords, variations (sabre, broadsword, cutlass, scimitar, etc.), much more. 336pp. 6⅛ × 9¼. 25434-8 Pa. $8.95

AUTOBIOGRAPHY: The Story of My Experiments with Truth, Mohandas K. Gandhi. Boyhood, legal studies, purification, the growth of the Satyagraha (nonviolent protest) movement. Critical, inspiring work of the man responsible for the freedom of India. 480pp. 5⅜ × 8½. (USO)   24593-4 Pa. $7.95

CELTIC MYTHS AND LEGENDS, T. W. Rolleston. Masterful retelling of Irish and Welsh stories and tales. Cuchulain, King Arthur, Deirdre, the Grail, many more. First paperback edition. 58 full-page illustrations. 512pp. 5⅜ × 8½.
                                                                    26507-2 Pa. $9.95

THE PRINCIPLES OF PSYCHOLOGY, William James. Famous long course complete, unabridged. Stream of thought, time perception, memory, experimental methods; great work decades ahead of its time. 94 figures. 1,391pp. 5⅜ × 8½. 2-vol. set.
                                                            Vol. I: 20381-6 Pa. $12.95
                                                            Vol. II: 20382-4 Pa. $12.95

THE WORLD AS WILL AND REPRESENTATION, Arthur Schopenhauer. Definitive English translation of Schopenhauer's life work, correcting more than 1,000 errors, omissions in earlier translations. Translated by E. F. J. Payne. Total of 1,269pp. 5⅜ × 8½. 2-vol. set.   Vol. 1: 21761-2 Pa. $10.95
                                                            Vol. 2: 21762-0 Pa. $11.95

MAGIC AND MYSTERY IN TIBET, Madame Alexandra David-Neel. Experiences among lamas, magicians, sages, sorcerers, Bonpa wizards. A true psychic discovery. 32 illustrations. 321pp. 5⅜ × 8½. (USO)   22682-4 Pa. $8.95

THE EGYPTIAN BOOK OF THE DEAD, E. A. Wallis Budge. Complete reproduction of Ani's papyrus, finest ever found. Full hieroglyphic text, interlinear transliteration, word-for-word translation, smooth translation. 533pp. 6½ × 9¼.
                                                                    21866-X Pa. $9.95

MATHEMATICS FOR THE NONMATHEMATICIAN, Morris Kline. Detailed, college-level treatment of mathematics in cultural and historical context, with numerous exercises. Recommended Reading Lists. Tables. Numerous figures. 641pp. 5⅜ × 8½.   24823-2 Pa. $11.95

THEORY OF WING SECTIONS: Including a Summary of Airfoil Data, Ira H. Abbott and A. E. von Doenhoff. Concise compilation of subsonic aerodynamic characteristics of NACA wing sections, plus description of theory. 350pp. of tables. 693pp. 5⅜ × 8½.   60586-8 Pa. $13.95

THE RIME OF THE ANCIENT MARINER, Gustave Doré, S. T. Coleridge. Doré's finest work; 34 plates capture moods, subtleties of poem. Flawless full-size reproductions printed on facing pages with authoritative text of poem. "Beautiful. Simply beautiful."—*Publisher's Weekly.* 77pp. 9¼ × 12.   22305-1 Pa. $5.95

NORTH AMERICAN INDIAN DESIGNS FOR ARTISTS AND CRAFTS-PEOPLE, Eva Wilson. Over 360 authentic copyright-free designs adapted from Navajo blankets, Hopi pottery, Sioux buffalo hides, more. Geometrics, symbolic figures, plant and animal motifs, etc. 128pp. 8⅜ × 11. (EUK)   25341-4 Pa. $7.95

SCULPTURE: Principles and Practice, Louis Slobodkin. Step-by-step approach to clay, plaster, metals, stone; classical and modern. 253 drawings, photos. 255pp. 8⅛ × 11.   22960-2 Pa. $9.95

CATALOG OF DOVER BOOKS

THE INFLUENCE OF SEA POWER UPON HISTORY, 1660–1783, A. T. Mahan. Influential classic of naval history and tactics still used as text in war colleges. First paperback edition. 4 maps. 24 battle plans. 640pp. 5⅜ × 8½.
25509-3 Pa. $12.95

THE STORY OF THE TITANIC AS TOLD BY ITS SURVIVORS, Jack Winocour (ed.). What it was really like. Panic, despair, shocking inefficiency, and a little heroism. More thrilling than any fictional account. 26 illustrations. 320pp. 5⅜ × 8½.
20610-6 Pa. $7.95

FAIRY AND FOLK TALES OF THE IRISH PEASANTRY, William Butler Yeats (ed.). Treasury of 64 tales from the twilight world of Celtic myth and legend: "The Soul Cages," "The Kildare Pooka," "King O'Toole and his Goose," many more. Introduction and Notes by W. B. Yeats. 352pp. 5⅜ × 8½. 26941-8 Pa. $7.95

BUDDHIST MAHAYANA TEXTS, E. B. Cowell and Others (eds.). Superb, accurate translations of basic documents in Mahayana Buddhism, highly important in history of religions. The Buddha-karita of Asvaghosha, Larger Sukhavativyuha, more. 448pp. 5⅜ × 8½.
25552-2 Pa. $9.95

ONE TWO THREE . . . INFINITY: Facts and Speculations of Science, George Gamow. Great physicist's fascinating, readable overview of contemporary science: number theory, relativity, fourth dimension, entropy, genes, atomic structure, much more. 128 illustrations. Index. 352pp. 5⅜ × 8½. 25664-2 Pa. $8.95

ENGINEERING IN HISTORY, Richard Shelton Kirby, et al. Broad, nontechnical survey of history's major technological advances: birth of Greek science, industrial revolution, electricity and applied science, 20th-century automation, much more. 181 illustrations. ". . . excellent . . ."—Isis. Bibliography. vii + 530pp. 5⅜ × 8¼.
26412-2 Pa. $14.95

Prices subject to change without notice.

Available at your book dealer or write for free catalog to Dept. GI, Dover Publications, Inc., 31 East 2nd St., Mineola, N.Y. 11501. Dover publishes more than 500 books each year on science, elementary and advanced mathematics, biology, music, art, literary history, social sciences and other areas.